KNOW WHERE YOU STAND

DIVORCE, SEPARATION, DE FACTO RELATIONSHIPS & THE FAMILY LAW SYSTEM

IAN SHANN

ACCREDITED FAMILY LAW SPECIALIST

SLATER & GORDON NATIONAL PRACTICE GROUP LEADER

AND

THE TEAM OF FAMILY LAW EXPERTS

AT SLATER & GORDON LAWYERS

WP

Published by:

WP Wilkinson Publishing Pty Ltd
ACN 006 042 173
Level 4, 2 Collins Street, Melbourne, Vic 3000
Tel: 03 9654 5446, www.wilkinsonpublishing.com.au
Copyright © 2011 Slater & Gordon Limited. All rights reserved.

National Library of Australia Cataloguing-in-Publication data:
Author:	Shann, Ian.
Title:	Know where you stand : with divorce, separation, de facto
	relationships & the family law system / Ian Shann.
ISBN:	9781921804595 (pbk.)
Subjects:	Australia. Family Law Act 1975.
	Separation (Law)--Australia.
	Divorce--Law and legislation--Australia.
Dewey Number:	346.940166
Cover Design:	Spike	Layout: Chris Georgiou

PREFACE

I was a 'victim' of the family law system before I became a family lawyer some 20 odd years ago.

Separated with three young children, my then wife decided on legal advice to fight financial matters in the Family Court. So I got my legal qualifications updated and handled my own case. We did manage to get the issues settled – after more than a year in the courts and many wasted dollars. On one occasion, the lawyer representing my wife lectured me over the telephone about what the husband had done (without the slightest basis in fact); obviously she did not realise that I was the person she was referring to. That experience gave me an insight into how 'the game is played' and how unpleasant the family law process can be.

Twenty years as a family lawyer and daily involvement in the experiences of many thousands of clients has simply confirmed for me how unpleasant and confusing the legal process can be, especially for those who don't know the system. Add to that the emotional impact of conflict and the uncertainty that goes with not knowing how the family law system works.

Having been drawn into the family law system as a client and, subsequently, as a family lawyer, I am convinced that we lawyers can and should do it much better and in a much more 'client-oriented' way. After all, as my wife, Janie, often tells me, "It's all about your clients – it's their court, not yours. The law is for them, not for you lawyers". Our job is simply to find an effective solution at a reasonable price.

Getting into a relationship is relatively easy in Australia. You and your partner just decide what you want to do ... and you do it.

However, whether you are married or in a de facto relationship (heterosexual or same-sex), getting out of that relationship may be a difficult experience – especially if you have children or you can't agree over the distribution of your property.

This book provides useful and practical information for those who find themselves involved in family law. It is written for those who do not know, or are unsure, what that law is and how it is applied.

There is only one family law in Australia – and this book tells you in very simple language what that law is, how it operates and how it might affect you if you have a breakdown in your relationship.

It takes you through the steps from separation until it's all over, with explanations in plain English and using simple diagrams. At the back of the book are additional resources and explanations of legal terms that might be relevant to you.

The book is very relevant for all couples, whether married, unmarried, gay, lesbian or transsexual, especially given recent changes in family law in Australia.

This book came about from a realisation that many people don't really understand what family law is about and how it might apply in their specific circumstances, and even fewer understand how family law legal fees and costs are calculated and charged and what the potential financial obligations might be.

Not all lawyers use plain language to explain the legal process or the options available. Lawyers also aren't good about discussing what their clients may end up paying for their services. *Know Where You Stand* explains family law and cost issues, step by step, in everyday language. It explains the reality of legal costs in family law and the steps you can take to minimise or, at very least, contain and control costs. This information could save you money that would otherwise end up in the pockets of lawyers or wasted on experts telling you what you already know.

Know Where You Stand provides a guide to:

▸   the legal principles when children are involved

▸   what is a fair and reasonable property settlement

▸   how to resolve matters as amicably as possible

▸   how and when to make an agreement that excludes the Family Court's powers

▸   the legal and court processes, step by step

▸   what to consider when deciding whether you need a lawyer

▸   how to find the right lawyer, what questions you should ask and how to instruct them, and

▸   how to get certainty and contain your legal costs.

It also lists useful resources and how to find them, and mentions some notable cases relevant to the issues we cover.

Know Where You Stand does not pretend to give you all the legal possibilities and all of the answers. It does not provide legal advice and **is not intended as a substitute for legal advice**. However, it is a guide that will help you to negotiate the processes involved and find appropriate advice when it might be needed.

In effect, it gives you a road map, showing the routes to follow in the family law process.

The original objectives for family law – to deliver justice in a quick, efficient and affordable way – should be honoured. But this can only happen if people who are involved in the system are empowered with the knowledge of how family law works and what it costs.

Know Where You Stand gives you that power.

Ian Shann

ACKNOWLEDGMENTS

Contributions to the writing of any book are necessarily many and varied.

I am grateful to Rod Cunich, Slater & Gordon's National Practice Group Leader (Business & Private Clients) and Harold Abrahams for getting the book started.

I also acknowledge the ongoing support and contributions made by Slater & Gordon's family law team members. The firm has family lawyers dotted throughout Australia and they have made a collective contribution to the development and production of *Know Where You Stand*. In particular, I thank Eliza Tiernan-Rose and Matt Bilsborough who have assisted greatly with research and detail and Monique Athanasiadies for countless drafts.

Others have made constructive suggestions and contributions to different parts of the book – mostly with good humour, especially the Melbourne mob led by Steven Edward and comprising Chris, Kelly, Mona, Mark, Eliza, Matt and Monique, Mel and Michelle, all of whom I have the pleasure of spending many of my working hours with.

Kalle Amanatides of Slater & Gordon's Marketing Department contributed enthusiastically to the creative process and production of the book. So, too, did bCreative (Slater & Gordon's marketing consultants) who were always on hand to provide insightful suggestions.

I take full responsibility for what is written in *Know Where You Stand* despite their contributions, no one else can be held accountable for the final result and the opinions expressed.

CONTENTS

INTRODUCTION

Everybody knows someone who is separating or divorcing. It is a fact of life in Australia today.

Until the 1970s, almost everyone living together in a relationship was married. Less than 10 per cent of marriages ended in divorce.

The *Family Law Act* 1975 for the first time introduced 'no-fault divorce' based on 12 months' separation. It is simply referred to in this book as the *Family Law Act*.

By 2011, the divorce rate was over 40 per cent and almost two million Australians lived in de facto relationships, many of them same-sex relationships. Thousands of de facto couples split up every year.

Before the *Family Law Act*, a divorce could only be granted by a court sitting in open session. These were public affairs and the private lives of divorcing couples were reported widely in the press. Before the *Family Law Act*, you had to get a divorce to finalise property settlement or to make arrangements about children. Unmarried and un-divorced couples were denied access to the courts for property settlements or protection of children.

THE FAMILY LAW ACT

If you are interested, you can find the Family Law Act at
www.austlii.edu.au/au/legis/cth/consol_act/fla1975114/

The *Family Law Act* is the cornerstone of Australia's family law system, providing one law throughout Australia that deals with people in all types of relationships. It enables arrangements to be made for children and property distribution after separation – whether you have been married or not.

POSITION IN WESTERN AUSTRALIA

Western Australia is the only Australian state to set up its own court to administer family law – the Family Court of Western Australia. The court deals with married people, de facto relationships and children's issues. In 1997 Western Australia passed legislation to include de facto relationships and children of parties who were not married.

The differences between Western Australia and the rest of Australia are:

▶ *In all other states, family law matters are dealt with by two federal courts: the Family Court of Australia and the Federal Magistrates Court.*

▶ *The Family Court of Western Australia combines the functions of the Family Court (with judges) and a Magistrates Court (with Magistrates).*

▶ *The WA Family Court is responsible for adoption applications. Elsewhere in Australia, adoption is dealt with by either the Supreme or District Courts of each state and territory.*

▶ *This court also has jurisdiction under the Surrogacy Act 2008 (WA) to make parentage orders (transferring parentage of a child from birth parents to arranged parents, who will later become the child's legal parents).*

We refer to 'family law' throughout this book to include not just children's and property matters but also child support and other related issues covered by legislation other than the *Family Law Act*.

We refer to the 'court' and the 'Family Courts' as any court that has jurisdiction to deal with matters under the *Family Law Act*, including the family court of Australia, the Federal Magistrates Court and the Family Court of Western Australia. For convenience, we also use the word 'judge' to describe the person who might be presiding over the court, although this might be a Magistrate, a Registrar or, in some cases, a Justice of the Peace.

SYMBOLS USED IN THIS BOOK

Tips

Information

Notable Cases

Caution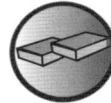

Resources

WHEN IT'S OVER, IT'S OVER - WHAT DO I DO NOW?

SUMMARY

▶ Think seriously about whether or not to leave a relationship.

▶ If you intend to leave, consider how you will leave, what you will take with you and what will happen to your children and your financial situation.

▶ Before you leave, make sure you have copies of all your important documents, as well as photos of valuable assets such as artwork and furniture.

▶ When you leave, take with you any items of personal importance. You may never see them again otherwise.

▶ Remember that every case is different – what happened in your sister's divorce, or your workmate's separation, is unlikely to be the same for you.

▶ You do not have to leave your home to separate from your partner. It is enough to say that you believe the relationship is over and that there is no prospect you will get back together.

▶ Stay safe. If you fear abuse or violence, there are many resources listed in this book to help. Remember, not all abuse is physical violence – abuse can be psychological or financial.

▶ Consider talking to a lawyer to figure out what your options are and where you stand. Even if you do not want to engage a lawyer throughout the process, it may help at the start so you can get your questions answered.

Leaving a relationship is not an easy decision

Whether to stay in a relationship or go is not a decision to make lightly, especially if you have children.

Perhaps the book *Too Good to Leave, Too Bad to Stay* (sub-titled *A Step-by-Step Guide to Help You Decide Whether to Stay or Get Out of Your Relationship*) by American psychotherapist Mira Kirshenbaum might assist. From time to time, most people have a question or two about their relationship. That's pretty normal. However, Kirshenbaum writes about the shift from being in a taken-for-granted relationship to trying to figure out whether to stay or leave.

Other books (among many) that might help include:

▸   *The Seven Principles for Making Marriage Work* by John Gottman

▸   *Men are from Mars, Women are from Venus* by John Gray

▸   *After the Affair* by Janis and Michael Spring

▸   *Getting the Love you Want* by Harville Hendrix

Whether yours is a marriage or a de facto relationship, once you have made the decision to separate – but before you actually do – you should plan your course of action.

Naturally, you will need to work out where you will go and when ... and with whom and with what. You might consider questions such as:

▸   Will you take the children?

▸   What about the pets?

▸   Do you fear a violent response?

▸   Can you take the company car?

▸   Does your departure create any legal implications?

It is important to get proper advice on these issues before you go, because your decisions may have unforeseen consequences that could cause problems for you in the future. If you are uncertain, seek assistance or support from one of several government agencies, counselling services or groups who can provide help. Most are either free or are reasonably priced and cost effective.

Some of these resources are set out in the pages that follow. If a particular resource is not helpful for you, they will at least give you guidance and point you in the right direction.

COUNSELLING SERVICES

*Counselling services that may be valuable to you in times of stress include Family Relationships Online at **www.familyrelationships.gov.au***
This Federal Government service exists to assist families to:
" … manage relationship issues, including agreeing on appropriate arrangements for children after parents separate."

You also need to determine whether you need to get legal advice at this stage (see chapter 9 'Lawyers – Finding the right ones and working with them'.

Making sure you have the information

When you separate, make sure you have access to information and documentation that may be useful to help resolve issues down the track. This information could be invaluable evidence if things can't be resolved sensibly.

For example, if you have a dispute over property, you will need to have access to information that might help a court to determine:

▶   What are your assets and liabilities?

▶   Who made what contribution to those assets and liabilities during your relationship and before you got together?

▶   What are your employment arrangements?

▶   Do either of you (or your children) have significant health issues?

▶   What are the care arrangements for your children?

Think about the information that might be available to you before you separate. Make a list of all of the assets in the home. If possible, take dated photographs of each room. Take photos of paintings, jewellery, antiques and any other precious items you may have. This will help demonstrate that the particular assets existed at that date (or use the age-old technique of including the front page of a newspaper in your photos). Take photographs of the inside of properties and gardens, to prove what condition they were in when you separated. You might be surprised how quickly people's recollections change about how well (or badly) properties have been maintained.

Copy or scan as many documents as you can, including:

▸   mortgage, lease or loan contracts

▸   bank and credit card statements, cheque and receipt book butts

▸   letters from business associates, financiers, banks, accountants or lawyers

▸   receipts for major items such as school fees, travel, furniture, electronics, building work and supplies, insurance

▸   pay slips and information about superannuation, and

▸   shareholding portfolios and property investments.

If you can't copy or scan documents, take a blank deposit form or a cheque to identify the bank and the branch where the accounts are held.

If you are in doubt about the relevance of any information you find, photograph it or copy it anyway. Better to have too much than too little.

You might also consider having images taken of computer hard drives (especially where computer information is pass-worded). A simple internet search will give you the details of companies that can perform this service for a reasonable fee. Having a copy of information held on computers may save you thousands of dollars in search costs and legal fees later on. A court can order that passwords be provided to enable you to access information from computer hard drives you have copied.

Gathering information is vital and, if matters get difficult, taking these precautions will almost certainly save you considerable legal and accounting fees. It can cost a great deal to get details of assets if your ex-partner decides to be unco-operative. The more information you have, the easier it will be. It can also help to negotiate a settlement much earlier if you are in possession of all the facts – and settlement is what you want to achieve, rather than waste your hard-earned earnings on legal fees.

Before separation – a bit of preliminary advice might help

When relationships are doing it tough, there is usually a lot of support and advice from the sidelines. Family and friends are there to help and often feel they are competent to advise you on what to do (or what not to do). However, the experiences of your sister-in-law, who was left by her husband five years ago and who had to fight tooth and nail to gain custody of the children, may not be relevant to your situation. The fact that your best friend got 65 per cent of the property distribution does not mean that you will.

Every case is different in family law. No two situations are the same. 'This is what happened' stories in family law matters are often distorted, one-sided or simply fail to mention matters that may have had a significant impact on the result.

Your family or friends can provide emotional support at this time but they are unlikely to be able to contribute much information of real value about family law and how it works, so be careful about acting on their advice on legal issues. It may well be inaccurate and cause more problems than are solved.

The breakdown of a relationship of any sort is usually pretty emotional. However, emotional issues – no matter how strongly you feel about the treatment you may have received, or the injustice of what your former partner has done – should not be allowed to cloud the real reason you are getting legal advice. You have a legal problem to resolve and it will be resolved faster (and at less cost) if you get into the facts of the matter and towards resolution rather than blame.

That is why a lawyer should stand back from emotion, look at the facts and apply their knowledge and experience to advise you what should be done. A lawyer can (and should) point you in the direction of a counsellor for psychological and emotional support to help you through these difficult times if that is what you need.

It is important that everyone going through the trials of a separation or divorce seeks independent professional advice, at least about:

▸   family law as it applies to your specific circumstances

▸   the legal processes you may have to go through

▸   your options and which course of action might be appropriate, and

▸   the costs and expenses involved.

Initial legal advice will usually be quite inexpensive (many family lawyers offer free first consultations) and it should give you a solid grounding about the system, what to expect and how much it's all going to cost. A good lawyer should also alert you to potential pitfalls and help you avoid making decisions you might regret later. Your lawyer can often point you in the right direction for additional assistance you might require.

What is separation?

Separation is a state of fact. You do not have to make a sworn statement or file documents in court to separate. Although it may have legal consequences, there is no such thing in Australia as a 'legal separation'.

The simplest demonstration of separation is a statement by one or both parties that the relationship is over and that there is no prospect of reconciliation. If necessary, document the position by giving the other person a note to that effect.

Separation can also be demonstrated by the way people behave. Evidence of separation could be when you no longer behave as a couple in a relationship even though you are still living in the same house. Physical separation, when one person leaves the home, is the most obvious evidence of an intention to end the relationship.

Interim financial arrangements

In short:

> Do you need money to support yourself but there are no kids?
> See spousal maintenance below.

> Do you need money to support your children?
> See ongoing child maintenance on page 7.

> Are you worried your ex is going to sell the house from under you?
> See injunctions to preserve property on page 7.

> Do you just need money for everyday living, or to pay your lawyers?
> See partial property settlement on page 7.

Spousal maintenance

If you are struggling to make ends meet because you have split up with a partner who provided financial support for many years, but is no longer prepared to continue that support, you may be able to obtain an order for spousal maintenance from the courts. Spousal maintenance orders will not be made in every situation.

The test to determine whether you should receive (or pay) financial support is in three parts. Firstly, whether you are unable to support yourself adequately without maintenance (hint: if the two of you are equally broke or struggling financially, the answer is likely to be 'no'). Secondly, whether the payer is reasonably able to pay. Thirdly, whether it would be proper for the payment to be made in the circumstances. The first step is really asking whether you have the capacity to earn sufficient income to support yourself; you will not be compelled to sell assets for this purpose.

If you were in a de facto relationship, you may be eligible for spousal maintenance on the same basis. Although the word 'spousal' is used, this is not limited to married couples.

Ongoing child maintenance

You can seek financial support for children in your care by applying to the Child Support Agency (CSA). See chapter 5 'It's only fair – child support' to find out how to do this.

However, if you want more than the amount assessed by the CSA, you will need to look to an arrangement outside the CSA. You are most likely to succeed if you want a specific cost paid, such as school fees or medical expenses – in addition to, or as part of, the CSA-assessed amount. This is the sort of complicated area of family law that will be particularly difficult to handle without a lawyer.

Injunctions to preserve property

In this context, an injunction is an order from a court that says STOP! You might, for example, get an injunction to prevent your ex-partner from selling off or dumping assets that you have an interest in. This extends to selling a house, shares or any other asset. The injunction will protect the property until the court determines (or you agree) how much and which items you will keep or what will be sold.

Partial property settlement

On the other hand, you may want to sell some of your property before court proceedings, to pay legal costs or for your own financial needs while the matter is being resolved. This should first be negotiated with the other party if at all possible, rather than through an application to court. It may be easier if property is sold to provide for both of your legal costs.

Once you have separated

Under family law, once you have separated, you can make arrangements for the distribution of your property and the living and time-sharing arrangements for your children. You don't have to wait around for the 12-month separation period to get matters resolved; 12 months of separation is simply the qualifying period for a divorce.

Property and children's arrangements may be finalised by coming to a settlement with your ex, or you can make an application to a court (see chapters 2 'Understanding the basics of family law', and 6 'Getting it settled – it's in your interests' for more details).

You could say goodbye, shut the door behind you ... then head straight down to the court to lodge an application. However, this is usually not the best option. The process of getting sound advice and deciding what to do next requires cool, calm thought.

In many cases, there is no crushing urgency about resolving matters. In others, there may be reasons to get things moving, such as protecting your children or ensuring assets are not sold or thrown away. Either way, it is wise to get some professional advice about your position and how best to move forward.

You may need to engage a lawyer at this point, or simply get some preliminary advice to help you work out your own resolution. If you have not obtained advice before separation, you certainly should do so soon afterwards. Your lawyer is there to give you advice and, if you choose to retain him or her, must act on your instructions. A lawyer cannot just take off on a wild goose chase of their own.

Getting advice (even legal advice) is not an aggressive or hostile thing to do, although many people see it that way when they discover their ex-partner has visited a lawyer. There is absolutely no reason why people who are separated (or in the process of separating) should not seek independent legal advice about their rights and how to deal with matters properly. Failing to get advice is a bit like hopping behind the wheel of a car without ever having learned to drive. You've seen other people do it, many of your friends may have told you about it, but if you have never driven a car before it might be sensible to get a few hints about driving, even if it's just so you can avoid crashing at the first bend.

If circumstances permit, be open. Tell your partner that you are simply trying to find out how to do things properly, not looking for ways to screw them for their last cent. What is important at this stage is that you are aware of your rights and responsibilities and have a framework to sort out the end of your relationship.

Some guiding principles:

▸ You do not have to have a disagreement with your ex-partner over what is going to happen with the children.

▸ You do not have to engage in a legal battle over the assets (or what will be left of them after you pay the legal expenses).

▸ You do not have to go to court.

However, what you **really should** do is find out where you stand and get some legal advice on your options and the best way to move forward.

Violence and abuse

You may be forced to leave home suddenly because of violence or abuse.

Abuse takes many forms. It can be physical, sexual or mental or a combination of any or all. None are acceptable in our society.

If you are the victim of violence, or have a real fear of violence occurring, contact the police or go to a Magistrates Court to apply for an order against the perpetrator. However, be absolutely sure that your claims are soundly based and are not just getting back at your partner. The courts do not approve of untrue stories about a violent partner that have been made up in order to gain some other advantage (such as sole occupation of the home or restrictions on contact with children). False claims about violence are a gross abuse of the legal process and can result in a costs order against you.

There are organisations in each state that provide support and assistance to victims of abuse or violence. Your lawyer can provide you with a list or you can find them on the internet.

If you have been abused in any way, note the details, including the time and date of the incidents and whether anybody else was present. Try to note what was said. If you have suffered injury, consult a doctor and ask for a report. Obtain photographic evidence where appropriate. Make a report to the police.

Your personal safety is paramount and you should do all in your power to avoid situations that may lead to abuse. Regrettably, all too often this is not possible.

COUNSELLING SUPPORT

Family violence
Australian Domestic & Family Violence Clearinghouse
www.austdvclearinghouse.unsw.edu.au
Domestic Violence Crisis Service ACT
www.dvcs.org.au
Domestic Violence Resource Centre Victoria
www.dvirc.org.au

For women
Information and support for mothers
www.women.gov.au
Women's Legal Service Victoria
www.communitylaw.org.au/women

For men
Men's Line Australia
www.menslineaus.org.au
Information and support for fathers
www.dadsindistress.asn.au
Support for step dads
www.stepdad.org

Mental Health & Counselling
Family Relationship Advice Line 1800 050 321
Lifeline 13 11 14
www.lifeline.org.au
www.blackdoginstitute.org.au
www.beyondblue.org.au
www.sane.org
www.healthfirst.net.au
www.shfpact.org.au

For counselling services Australia-wide
www.aifs.gov.au/nch/nchhelp
Parentline, 24-hour, free telephone counselling1300 130 052
www.parentline.org.au
Lifeworks Relationship Counselling & Education Services (Anglican)
email lifeworks@lifeworks.com.au

SHELTERS, REFUGES & CRISIS CENTRES

A list of hotlines, shelters, refuges and crisis centres is available at
www.hotpeachpages.net/auspac/aus.html

Financial abuse

There has been much discussion in recent times about the concept of 'financial abuse' – the use of financial dominance as a tool to extract an advantage from other people. Examples of financial abuse may include withholding access to finances, and comments such as "You will get nothing if you leave," or "Unless you ... I will close the bank accounts and cancel your credit cards," or "Get out of the house, take the children and see what you can get from Centrelink."

Steps to introduce financial abuse into the Family Law Act

Late in 2010, a Bill proposing substantial changes to the definition of family violence in the *Family Law Act* was introduced into Federal Parliament. The Bill – which is called Family Law Legislation Amendment (Family Violence and Other Measures) 2011 – makes the definition of family violence much broader. One of the elements that is proposed is financial abuse.

Financial abuse is included within the broader definition of 'family violence' as:

Unreasonably denying [a] family member the financial autonomy that he or she would otherwise have had; or

Unreasonably withholding financial support needed to meet the reasonable living expenses of the family member, or his or her child, at a time when the family member is entirely or predominantly dependent on the person for financial support.

This change would make financial withholding from a former partner or children, a much more damaging claim. This is not simply because it is defined as violence, but because of the way violence is treated more generally in family law.

However, at the time of writing, the Bill had not been passed by the Parliament – we will have to wait and see what happens.

A FEW PRACTICAL TIPS

▸ Take photos of your personal property, especially if you are leaving the joint home.

▸ Make copies (or retain originals) of all financial documents and keep them in a safe place.

▸ Don't move out of the home until you have had legal advice.

▸ Obtain legal advice before starting detailed negotiations about property. You may make an agreement that is unfair to you without knowing it.

▸ Don't try to prevent your children from having contact with their other parent unless there are issues of violence or abuse.

▸ Visit your children's school and speak to teachers to let them know the separation has occurred. Schools need to know so they can help monitor the children's adjustment to separation.

▸ Keep a diary. If a matter proceeds to court, you may need to prepare an affidavit detailing issues relating to the children's arrangements. People often find it difficult to remember timelines and dates. Keeping a diary will make it easier. Include notes about contact dates with your children, even those that are missed.

▸ If you are struggling with your grief reactions at the time of separation, your GP can refer you under Medicare for six sessions with a registered psychologist.

▸ Talk to friends and family members for support.

▸ Get professional help to deal with the emotional fall-out – for example, from a psychologist.

▸ Be open minded about counselling for yourself and for your children. Even if your partner is reluctant to attend counselling, you may find it very helpful to attend on your own.

UNDERSTANDING THE BASICS
OF FAMILY LAW

SUMMARY

▶ Family law is not complicated.

▶ The objectives of family law are straight forward:

- to protect the best interests of any children, and

- to provide for a fair and reasonable split of your property.

▶ Most of the time, there are two options when your relationship is over – settle matters between you, or take your case to court and fight over who gets what.

▶ Going to court is a very expensive and negative process.

▶ The requirements for obtaining a divorce are very straightforward – 12 months separation.

▶ If you are in a relationship and live together, you might be in a legal de facto relationship (including if your relationship is a same-sex relationship).

▶ If you are in a de facto relationship and you break up, the court will treat your relationship as if it was a marriage. Dividing up your assets would be dealt with the same way.

▶ Children of de facto relationships are also covered by family law.

What family law is … and is not

Family law is not complex or difficult. Basically, it deals with issues around children and property (financial matters) after you have separated.

Family law provides for:

▶ what happens after you separate (whether married or in a de facto relationship)

▶ how you divide up what was previously owned by both of you, and

▶ how arrangements are made for your children (including child support).

That's it – family law provides for financial distribution and arrangements for your children. Family law also enables you to formally end a marriage by divorce.

The *Family Law Act* was originally passed to create an informal court with the power to deliver justice at reasonable cost, quickly and compassionately – and enable people to get on with their lives after separation. 'Fault' and 'blame' were removed from family law in 1975.

Since 1975, the *Family Law Act* has become a much more complex set of laws. But the bottom line remains: the law is in place to enable people who have separated to resolve the distribution of their property on a fair and reasonable basis and put in place arrangements that are in the best interests of their children.

De facto relationships

Since March 2009, family law has included de facto relationships. Put simply, a 'de facto' is a person living in a relationship with another person (of any gender) as if they were married.

De facto relationships (including same-sex relationships), were once the domain of the various state laws and state courts. They are now covered by the Commonwealth *Family Law Act*.

In Western Australia, de facto relationships have been part of family law since 1997 and are dealt with in the Family Court of Western Australia. All other states (except South Australia) transferred their powers over de facto relationships to the Commonwealth and these became part of the *Family Law Act* on 1 March 2009. South Australia became part of the national arrangements on 1 July 2010.

If you separated as a de facto couple before the relevant date in the previous paragraph (WA – 1997, SA – 1 July 2010, everywhere else – 1 March 2009), your relationship would be covered by the laws of the state you live in. If you and your ex-partner agree, you may choose to be covered by the provisions of the *Family Law Act* and have your dispute dealt with in the Commonwealth Family Courts (except in Western Australia, where you are dealt with under the *Family Court Act* (W.A.).

The long and the short of this is that every domestic relationship in Australia is now effectively covered by the general family law. So, any disputes about property distribution, including superannuation (except in Western Australia, where de factos are not included in the super regime), or children's issues arising out of a de facto relationship are now dealt with under the Commonwealth *Family Law Act*.

What constitutes a de facto relationship?

To decide whether you are in a de facto relationship, the court will consider a list of elements that may or may not apply to you. None of the factors is, of itself, a deciding factor. The court might consider all of the factors, or none of them, or even some additional factor not on the list at all. Normally, you will have to have been in a relationship for two years to constitute a legal de facto relationship. However, it is also possible the court may define your relationship as de facto before this period has elapsed and, on the other side of the coin, you may have been together for much longer without being in a de facto relationship under family law.

A court will take into account:

- the length of your relationship (how long have you been together?)

- the nature and extent of your common residence (have you lived together at all and for how long?)

- whether a sexual relationship exists between you

- the degree of financial dependence or interdependence and any arrangements for financial support between you (how do you manage your money? together or separately?)

- the ownership, use and acquisition of your property (do you own property together?)

- the degree of mutual commitment to a shared life (are you committed to each other?)

> ▸ whether the relationship is registered under a state law

> ▸ the care and support of children (do you have kids? who looks after them?), and

> ▸ the reputation and public aspects of your relationship (do other people think you're a serious couple?)

ARE YOU IN A DE FACTO RELATIONSHIP?

A de facto relationship is one where two people "have a relationship as a couple (hetero or same sex) living together on a genuine domestic basis".
However…

> ▸ *Whether you are in a de facto relationship is a state of fact.*
> ▸ *You can be legally in a de facto relationship even if you don't think you are – even if you swear that you aren't and don't want to be.*
> ▸ *A de facto relationship can exist if either of you is legally married to someone else – or even if you or your partner is in another de facto relationship.*

A court may find that you are in a de facto relationship even if:

> ▸ *you have never shared a residence or spent consistent time sleeping at one another's homes or even had a sexual relationship with each other*
> ▸ *you have never co-mingled finances or displayed any intention to financially support one another, or*
> ▸ *you have only been together for a short period of time (less than a year) and do not have any children together.*

A recent case in the Family Court – while reaffirming that every case has to be determined in the light of its own particular situation and whether a de facto relationship exists is a state of fact – looked at a concept of 'coupledom' (the merging of partners' lives in such a way that they regarded themselves, and presented to the public, as a couple). In that case, the partners had a relationship of over 17 years, were sexually involved on a regular basis and one provided the other substantial financial support. However, the judge decided that they were not in a de facto relationship because there was not this essence of 'coupledom'.

There have been very few court cases determined under the *Family Law Act* since it applied to de factos in 2009, so it may be very much a matter of "watch this space" while the law develops and becomes clearer!

De facto includes same-sex relationships

At the time of writing (and despite much agitation for change), laws have not been passed in Australia to legitimise gay and lesbian relationships by marriage and give them the same status as traditional wedded partnerships. However, under family law, same-sex partners are otherwise treated the same way as any other de facto partnership.

Why is it important to define the relationship?

People in a de facto relationship now have the same financial responsibilities to their partners as if they were married. If you are in a de facto relationship, any disputes over your children or over property will be treated by law in the same way as for a married couple.

De facto couples end their relationships by separating in the same way as married couples. They do not need a separation declaration or any legal document to end the union. The fact of separation is no different to that of a married couple and, like married couples, you can be separated even if you continue to live under the one roof.

So, the chapters of this book on property and financial matters are very relevant for all couples, whether married or de facto and regardless of sexual orientation.

PARTNERS LIVING APART

A study by the Australian Institute of Family Studies in April 2011 revealed that around 1.1 million Australians are in committed relationships but living separately from their partner.

A significant number of these couples would probably be regarded as de facto couples under family law and, if they decided to end their relationships, would be subject to the same laws as those separating from a marriage.

Children of a de facto relationship

Children born to an unmarried couple have been covered by the *Family Law Act* since 1988.

Before the *Family Law Act* became law in 1975, children of unmarried parents were still stigmatised as being 'illegitimate'. At that time, it was common to hear children born out of wedlock described as 'bastards'. Today, illegitimate is more likely to refer to a breach of sporting rules and to be called a bastard is not necessarily a criticism in Australia. Having kids without being married is now commonplace and the proportion of children born to de facto couples is growing every year.

The chapters of this book about resolving children's issues apply to everyone with kids, whether you are de facto or married.

What family law covers

The objectives of family law are to ensure that the best interests of children are protected and that proper financial arrangements are made for the division of property. The *Family Law Act* and the decisions of the Family Courts set out the principles and rules for resolving those issues and other matters that might be involved, such as relocating children from one place to another, getting passports for children, how to deal with inheritances, superannuation or interests in a business.

The basic law is set out in the *Family Law Act*, which is then applied and clarified by decisions of the courts.

If you want to understand family law you need to understand not just the *Family Law Act* (and the other pieces of legislation that affect family law) but also the court decisions that may be relevant to the issues involved in your case. That is why – unless your matter is very straightforward – you may need the help of a lawyer.

Laws are written by, interpreted and applied by lawyers. Maybe that's why they can be so complex. To make it a bit more difficult, the most important family laws are discretionary, which means that a judge has a wide range of possibilities to choose from when determining arrangements for children or dividing up your property. Nothing is set in stone. There are no set formulas or rules to determine exactly what will be decided by the judge, either for property distribution or for arrangements for the children. Family law operates within broad guidelines.

Child support is also an important part of the broader family law. The child support system is designed to ensure that parents pay a reasonable amount for the care of their children after the breakdown of a relationship. The Child Support Agency (CSA) was established (initially as part of the Australian Taxation Office) to administer the system and distribute money from the paying parent to the receiving parent under formulas that have been modified over time.

'Fair and reasonable' and 'children's best interests'

> *"What you see and hear depends a good deal on where you are standing."*
> *– C.S. Lewis*

'Fair and reasonable financial arrangements' and a 'child's best interests' are the fundamental principles on which family law is based. These are pretty broad concepts and are capable of widely differing interpretations.

There is no right and wrong in family law. There are just differing perceptions, views and shades of grey. Disputes tend to get exaggerated in the emotional environment of a breakup, so try to stand back from the conflict, be objective and aim to see things through the eyes of others as well as your own.

If you get caught up in the correctness of your position or on a principle of who is right and who is wrong, your experience with the family law process is likely to be a long and unsatisfying one. If you have lawyers involved, it will also be expensive.

The family law system can only ever deliver a lose-lose result. You will always have less than you did before, because you are dividing up what was previously shared between you – whether it is your involvement with your children or the fruits of your financial endeavours.

Settling or going to court

The vast majority of people with family law issues do not want to get caught up in lengthy and expensive legal processes or in the courts. Most would prefer to get matters settled as quickly, inexpensively and amicably as is possible.

Family law exists to help you do just that, by encouraging you to make voluntary agreements to finalise financial and children's issues, or by providing a forum for making decisions on issues you are unable to resolve with your ex-partner.

In most situations you will choose how you resolve your post-separation issues – either by going to court or by resolving them, if you are able to do this directly with your ex-partner.

You can settle 'out of court' and, there are several ways of documenting an agreement and making it legal and effective. However, if you can't get things resolved, you may have to take your dispute to the Family Courts and ask a judge to rule on the issues.

If you have to go to court, you must follow the rules and regulations regarding court processes and procedures (these are dealt with in some detail in chapter 8 'If it positively, definitely has to go to court').

Even if you are already in the court process, you may still settle before the matter goes to a trial before a judge. Over 90 per cent of all cases that begin in the Family Courts are resolved before the trial, by agreement between the parties. If you do not resolve all of your issues, you may have to go to a trial to enable a judge to examine the issues and make a decision that will then be binding on everyone.

Finalisation by agreement

Getting matters settled by agreement and without court action is almost always in your best interests.

Court cases can take years rather than months, so settlement will achieve substantial savings in both time and legal costs. A fair and reasonable settlement provides certainty and allows you to get on with your life without the unpredictable outcome of the court process. Settlement also reduces the potential for ongoing conflict between you and your ex (and the inevitable impact of parental conflict on children) and the potential involvement of your wider family and friends.

If you and your ex are able to agree on your property division or children's matters, you have several choices:

- come to a private agreement with your ex-partner and follow through on it – whether you put it in writing or not

- draft up consent orders setting out your agreement and submit them to the court for approval (with or without legal assistance), or

- get a lawyer to prepare a Financial Agreement (for matters that only involve property and financial maintenance of your ex-partner or yourself).

If you want to resolve child support issues privately and without the intervention of the Child Support Agency, you can get a lawyer to prepare a Binding Child Support Agreement.

The advantages and disadvantages of each of these choices are dealt with in detail in chapters 5 'It's only fair – child support', 6 'Getting it settled – it's in your interests' and 7 'Contracting out of the family law system – Financial Agreements'.

Resolution by the courts or the Child Support Agency (CSA)

Sometimes matters ultimately have to go to court because:

▶ the parties simply cannot agree on proposals to resolve issues

▶ there are substantial differences about the facts (or the interpretation of facts) or because your ex-partner is just 'not playing ball'

▶ you are advised by your lawyer that it's in your interests to start the process to get the other party moving, or

▶ you may have an urgent need for the court to protect your children from harm or to preserve assets from being wasted or being sent outside the country.

Where agreement cannot be reached, you can make an application for the court to make decisions about property distribution and/or children's issues. You can do this with or without legal assistance. You can involve the Child Support Agency by making an application to the CSA for a determination of liability to pay child support (without legal assistance).

There are many and varied reasons that might justify starting legal proceedings in family law matters. However, going to court should always be your last resort.

Court processes are explained in detail in chapter 8 'If it positively, definitely has to go to court'.

Divorce

De facto couples do not need any court orders to confirm their separation or the end of their relationship. It is over when one or both decides that is the case.

Married couples must apply to the court to obtain a divorce. If the parties have been separated for at least 12 months it's usually pretty much a formality.

In this book, the word 'divorce' refers to the formal ending by a court of a relationship between a man and a woman who have been married.

The rate of divorce in Australia has dropped steadily over the past ten years. It is now under 50,000 a year. Research indicates that the majority of marriage separations were initiated by females. A significant number of people in this country live together as unmarried couples (de facto), but their breakups are not included in these statistics.

In Australia, it is now relatively easy to get a divorce. However, to do so, you must first prove that you were actually married. If you were married in Australia, this must have occurred in either a religious ceremony or a civil ceremony conducted by a celebrant (a person authorised by the government).

Are you married ... or not?

Answering this question is not a problem for most people. A large percentage of our resident population was not married in Australia. In many countries, a marriage is on the record and it is easy to obtain documentary evidence from the registry where the marriage took place. Some countries can be slow at providing the documentation. In other countries, where there have been wars or natural disasters, the records may no longer be available. So, make sure that you start getting the documentation as early as possible.

In some countries, there is no documentation, and evidence of a marriage will have to be provided (usually by affidavits or statements from both parties) before a divorce can be granted. In brief, if you were validly married under the laws of the country where the marriage took place, Australian law generally accepts the validity of that marriage. As an example, in Laos, a couple is properly married if they hold a party and declare before more than five relatives or friends that they want to spend the rest of their lives together. As far as Australian law is concerned, couples who have gone through this ceremony in Laos are married.

The Family Court has jurisdiction over your divorce if you are an Australian citizen or have been a resident in Australia for 12 months and ordinarily live in this country.

The legal age for marriage in Australia is 18 years for both males and females. However, in exceptional circumstances, the marriage of a person under 18 years of age but over 16 may be authorised by the court.

Annulment of a marriage

Annulment of a marriage is quite a different issue and is much more difficult to obtain than a divorce. A court will only make a declaration that a marriage is null and void in very limited circumstances. These include bigamous marriages or where the consent of a party to a marriage was obtained by fraud.

It may be possible to claim that you were not married because of a mistake about the identity of the person you married. However, if you thought that your future wife or husband was a person of incredible wealth, but this was not the case, that's tough. That is not mistaken identity, just mistaken expectations.

You might have a better chance if you did not understand 'the nature and consequences' of the ceremony you went through. Again, each case will depend on its own circumstances and a wide range of factors may be considered by the court in deciding whether or not, at the time you got married, you really understood what you were doing.

You may also be able to obtain an annulment if you were forced into a marriage against your will by threats or coercion.

Bigamy

Bigamy is the offence of marrying a person while already legally married to another person. If the first marriage is legal, number two is not. Under the *Marriage Act* a bigamist faces imprisonment for five years (as well as the wrath of two people). It would be a brave person who attempted 'trigamy' (the wrath of three).

If you were married in a country where multiple marriages are legal, all marriages valid in that country would be recognised as legal in Australia and it would be legal to bring all of your wives to Australia if you migrate.

Getting the divorce

There are very few contested divorces – where one person is opposed to the granting of the divorce. In any case, although it takes two people to get into a marriage, only one person needs to apply for a divorce. An Application for Divorce can also be made by both of you jointly.

To apply for a divorce, you must be in a position to prove all of the following:

▸ you are married (by providing a marriage certificate or other appropriate evidence of the relationship)

▸ you have been separated from your former partner for at least 12 months

▸ there is no reasonable prospect that you will get back together, and

▸ you or your spouse are Australian residents or citizens, or regard Australia as your permanent home.

If this is the case, you can file the relevant papers in the Family Court and, unless there are issues relating to the care of your children, you will get your divorce. In fact, you don't even need to attend court when the divorce is granted, unless there are children of the marriage under 18 years of age.

The dates of your separation and divorce are important when it comes to negotiating a property settlement.

If you are separated but not divorced, you can make an application regarding property or children's matters to the Family Courts straight away. Sometimes it is better to get all of your parenting and financial arrangements resolved before you apply for a divorce. You can bring an application regarding children's matters any time after a divorce, without restriction. However, after you get divorced, you have only a further 12 months to commence proceedings in the Family Courts regarding property (and that includes starting an Application for Consent Orders). After that time you cannot seek any orders from the court regarding property matters (this includes maintenance and financial support) unless you already have a prior application going or you get permission from the court to do so. In a de facto relationship, you can seek financial orders in the Family Courts up to 24 months from the date of your separation.

What is separation?

'Separation' is not defined in the *Family Law Act* – it is simply a state of fact that exists where one (or both) parties no longer consider themselves to be in a partnership and there is no reasonable prospect of reconciliation. You do not have to be living apart to be separated in the eyes of the law. You could be legally separated but still living 'under the one roof', as long as the conditions for separation have occurred.

The court will require affidavit evidence to verify you have been separated under the one roof in order to get a divorce. The court will look to evidence of the end of the relationship and consider domestic arrangements – for example, who does the shopping, cooking, washing and cleaning. You may have an ongoing financial relationship and still be separated by law.

There is a 'kiss and make up' provision in the *Family Law Act* that allows a separated couple to get back together for up to three months to try and make the relationship work without affecting the date of their original separation.

Effectively, the 12-month separation period is suspended during the 'kiss and make up' period. This can occur only once in any 12-month period. For example:

- ▶ 1 April 2010 – separation under the one roof.

- ▶ 1 July 2010 – 'kiss and make up' attempt begins.

- ▶ 1 September 2010 – 'kiss and make up' fails.

To qualify for a divorce, the separation would normally have been completed in April 2011 but the two months of 'kiss and make up' which failed, extends the 12 months' separation period to 1 June 2011. If you try to reunite more than once, the date of commencement of separation restarts.

Married less than two years or have children?

If you have been married for less than two years, you must attend counselling before a court will grant a divorce. The law requires attendance but does not demand a result. If you advise the court that you attended counselling, then you have complied with your legal obligations.

Before granting a divorce to a couple with children under the age of 18, the court must be satisfied that arrangements for the care of those children are appropriate.

A word about wills

When you get married, any existing will you may have made is automatically cancelled. If this happens, and you die without making a new will, your assets will be divided up according to state laws. Your estate may become the subject of a legal dispute between your relatives and those who think you should have made financial provision for them in your will.

In some states, your will is automatically revoked (cancelled) if you divorce. It is sensible to consult a lawyer to confirm what the position is in the state where you live. You may have already done a property settlement with your ex-partner but, because your will is still in place, that partner may get another share of what you leave behind.

Family Relationship Centres

Family Relationship Centres were established by the Federal Government to provide information and confidential advice to help parties resolve family disputes.

In children's matters, you must attend mediation before making any application in the Family Courts (unless there are exceptional circumstances). The Family Relationship Centres provide a service for this.

The Family Relationship Centre website provides all the details you need to know about its services and how it may be able to assist. Located throughout Australia, the centres are "staffed by independent, professionally qualified staff offering confidential and impartial services in a welcoming, safe and confidential environment".

The centres provide information, advice and dispute resolution (such as mediation) to help people reach agreement on parenting arrangements without going to court. They also offer individual, group and joint sessions to help separating families make workable arrangements for their children.

FAMILY RELATIONSHIP CENTRES

www.familyrelationships.gov.au/Services

IT'S ALL ABOUT THE KIDS – CHILDREN'S ISSUES

SUMMARY

▶ The basic principles set out in the *Family Law Act* for children are:

- kids have the right to be properly cared for and protected from harm, and

- parents have the responsibility to care for them.

▶ You will probably have to compromise around arrangements for your children. Try to be flexible about the arrangements – it will be better for you and, more importantly, much better for your children. Compromise involves not fighting over every single issue; not presenting a target often assists in reducing stress and tension.

▶ Try to keep lines of communication open in the negotiation phase and after you have resolved children's issues. There are many decisions to be made about your children's future; and, in almost all circumstances, you will have to consult each other about them.

▶ If your children's matters end up with lawyers or in the Family Courts, try to keep a sense of proportion about what is happening – it's pointless spending $2,500 on legal bills for an argument over who should be washing and returning the children's school clothes when you could buy a second set for one tenth of the legal expense.

▶ The way a court will see the children's situation may be quite different to the way you see it, or the way you would expect the court to see it.

▶ Each child is an individual and, as they grow older, the court will pay more attention to their personalities and opinions. When deciding where the children should live, a court is more likely to consider their opinion in their mid to late teens than when they are younger.

> ▸ If you want to move a long distance away from your partner, sharing time with your children will be difficult. These cases often end up in court because it is difficult to decide who the children should live with when the direct consequence is restricted contact with the other parent.

This chapter is about issues around children that are relevant in family law.

A child is a person who is under 18 years of age. The basic principle of the *Family Law Act* in relation to children has not changed since the Act was introduced in 1975: the best interests and welfare of the child are paramount.

An important part of family law is to provide a framework to make proper arrangements for children after their parents separate. These are commonly referred to as parenting orders. This term describes all court orders that deal with children's issues, whether made by consent (agreement) or by the court.

They can be simple:

> *"Lizzie and Michael shall spend equal time with their parents on alternate weeks commencing at 5:00 p.m. each Sunday."*

They may also be very complex. Such orders often cover specific arrangements about where the children are each minute of their lives, setting out who will be responsible for every aspect of their care and control (and who won't) and prescribing which schools, religious institutions and relatives they will be involved with (or not), where they are to be delivered and collected from when moving from one household to another, in what conveyance they are to travel and who is to supervise the handovers. The orders might even specify what the children are to be fed, what medication is to be administered, which clothes will travel with them (and in what condition), who they may telephone, when and at whose expense.

These are all 'parenting orders'.

The boring bit:

The laws for children's matters are set out in Part VII of the *Family Law Act*.

The difficult bit:

How do parents – who were previously living together and (more or less) making joint decisions about their kids – come to an agreement and continue to make decisions about these matters after they have separated and when they are living apart?

The practical bit:

Parents need to reach an agreement that resolves arrangements for the kids in a way that respects their children's interests and promotes their welfare. If they don't, or can't, do this, the courts will do it for them.

Two fundamental themes underlie family law as it relates to children:

▸ kids have the right to be properly cared for and protected from harm, and

▸ parents have the responsibility to care properly for their children.

This is what the *Family Law Act* provides and it is what the courts consistently order.

So, ask yourself:

"Do the arrangements advance the best interests of our children – or not?"

All separated parents must deal with, and resolve, this fundamental question.

While it is not always possible for parents to agree fully on what arrangements are best for their kids, most manage to reach an agreement they can live with – even though it might not be their number one preference. Remember that compromise is generally an essential ingredient in making arrangements for your children and co-operation is essential in order to make those arrangements work.

Compromise will reduce the levels of conflict and tension around children's issues. In turn, this should make life very much easier for all, especially the children. If you fight for every possible advantage and concede nothing, the conflict will go on and the stress levels will continue to rise.

Some issues can never be compromised, such as the physical and emotional safety of your children. However, try to be as objective as possible and keep in mind that the best interests of the children are what this is all about. Pick your fights wisely and dig your heels in only on really important issues.

The advantages of settling disputes apply to children's issues as they do to any other matters. Consider the cost, the time and the likely outcome and ask whether it's really worth going to court. Exhaust your avenues for negotiation and dispute resolution before you commence proceedings.

Arrangements for the kids

As a parent you have obligations towards your children – not rights.

The *Family Law Act* states that:

> *"The best interests of the child is the paramount consideration."*

The key issue is to work out what is in the best interests of the children, not the wishes of one parent or the other, grandparents, new partners or anyone else.

Until quite recently, 'custody' of children was awarded to one parent, with the other having 'access' and specified rights to see them. Under such arrangements, children were often fought over by the parents, with each side claiming that they were the one better equipped to have custody. Children were treated like pieces of property, the result being that custody was seen as the 'prize' for being the better parent. Sadly, some parents showed little interest in having regular access if they did not 'win' custody.

Over the years, other concepts and terminology have replaced 'custody' and 'access', including:

- ▶ 'residence' and 'contact', or
- ▶ 'living with' and 'spending time with'.

Despite the changes in language, the core principle has remained the same: "the best interests of the child should be the determining factor in deciding when and with whom children should live."

Deciding the arrangements for children

Getting it resolved by agreement

Today, couples who have decided to separate are encouraged to talk rationally about the effect their situation will have, and has had, on the children. Minimising the negative impact of living with two parents in different homes and at different times is extremely important. Therefore, if parents can decide on a mutual approach to bringing up the children, everyone will benefit. Decisions parents will have to make include:

- ▶ where the children will live (one place or two?)

- ▶ what religious celebrations and worship the children will take part in

- ▶ what type of education and schools the children should attend

- ▶ what attendance at sporting and extra-curricular activities is appropriate

- ▶ how to fit in with the parents' work arrangements,

- ▶ when and where the children should spend time with others (grandparents and other relatives)

- ▶ what the handover arrangements will be

- ▶ how to make arrangements for the children during holidays (school holidays and long weekends)

- ▶ what arrangements should be in place for birthdays, special and family celebrations

- ▶ whether the children have any special needs, including medical requirements

- ▶ what arrangements are reasonable for spending time with siblings and step siblings, and

- ▶ how to bring flexibility into the terms of the agreement to provide for future events.

When discussing arrangements for their children, parents should place a large notice in front of them that reads:

THE DECISIONS WE MAKE
ARE IN THE BEST INTERESTS OF OUR CHILDREN

Do not allow the children to become 'collateral damage' to the emotional fallout of your separation. They are not responsible for the split and parents have a responsibility to minimise any suffering they experience as a result of it. Your views about the children's best interests are very important, but they are only one person's view. Remember:

"What you see and hear depends a good deal on where you are standing."

Each parent probably has a different view of what is in the children's best interests. But it is not a matter of getting the other person to agree with those views. It is a matter of finding a path that will best serve the children's welfare.

Children's issues are not like engaging in wage and salary negotiations. Don't start with an ambit claim (an extreme position that is not sustainable), or pretend to seek conditions that you are really willing to sacrifice in exchange for others. To do so is only playing with your children's welfare. That kind of approach just puts your interests before those of your children and the 'game' is not likely to be successful. The other parent will likely respond to the tactic by taking a totally opposite position and you will end up too far apart for meaningful negotiations.

It is worthwhile thinking about what your worst-case scenario might be. For example, consider how little time the kids might end up spending with you if the matter goes to court and it all goes wrong?

If you think that is pretty bleak, the scenario could become even bleaker if you engage in an all-in court battle over children's issues. The more you fight, the less chance you will have of getting the matter resolved as you might wish – and the more expense you will incur. The final decisions will be made by a judge who (correctly) will take only the needs of the children into consideration, not yours.

EQUAL TIME – DOES IT REALLY MEAN 'EQUAL'?

Before the court makes a parenting order, it must consider whether equal time with each parent is practical and would be in the child's best interests.

It is presumed that 'equal shared care' is in a child's best interests unless it can be demonstrated otherwise. While this has not led to a situation where each parent will have the children living with them for exactly the same lengths of time, it has compelled the courts to consider the appropriateness of kids spending pretty much equal time with each parent – quite a change from the previous laws, which had no such requirement.

'Equal shared parental responsibility' – the parents' decision-making about their child or children – applies in all children's matters. Today, both parents have an equal say in parenting decisions, such as where the children will go to school, their eating and sleeping habits, their health, their religious observances etc. This is the case even if nobody seeks an order for equal shared parental responsibility.

Equal shared parental responsibility can be reversed where there are reasonable grounds to believe that a parent has abused the child or there has been family violence. It can also be overturned where the court is satisfied that this would be in the child's best interest.

Criticising the other parent (or their family)

A parent should not attempt to influence the children against the other parent or the other parent's family. Neither parent should use their children as pawns in battles over the spoils of a relationship that has ended or to inflict damage on the other. It is worth repeating: a parent does not stop being a parent simply because of separation.

Attitude towards responsibilities as a parent and towards the other

The attitude each parent shows (and has shown in the past) towards their responsibilities as a parent is an important factor in deciding what arrangements should be put in place for children.

While this is pretty obvious, when decisions are made about where the children will live, a parent who has demonstrated and continues to show a positive interest in the welfare of the children will be better placed than a parent who has not. That is not to suggest this is a competition to decide which parent has the 'best attitude'. Both parents can be positive and properly concerned about the children's welfare and demonstrate this through their actions. Equally, a parent who simply talks about how interested they are in their children's welfare but does little by way of practical activity will find it hard to convince a court that their proposals for the children are the best.

Another consideration is how each parent has promoted the relationship of the children with the other parent. So, if you prevent the children from having much to do with the other parent purely because of dislike or blame for the breakdown of the relationship, this is unlikely to advance your cause.

The age and stage of the kids

Arrangements for the children will often depend on their ages and their relationships with each other and usually have to be reconsidered as time moves on. For example, the day-to-day needs of a baby are very much tied to its mother. The Family Court is unlikely to remove a baby or toddler from the care of the mother on a long-term basis.

Social research has shown that, as a general rule, a younger child needs shorter but more frequent periods with the 'non-primary' parent (in traditional relationships, usually the male). As a child gets older, the periods can be longer and less frequent.

The wishes of a child are relevant in looking at what is in a child's best interests, especially as they get older. The courts are less likely to intervene and make any orders as a child gets close to their 18th birthday. So, if a 16-year-old boy wants to spend time going fishing or going to the footy with his father, the courts are unlikely to entertain an application that says he is not allowed to go because he should be spending time with his mother instead.

Education, religion and cultural issues

Schooling, religion and social and cultural backgrounds may be important considerations when negotiating arrangements for children. The issues will be different in every case but should be thought through carefully before orders are sought (whether by consent or in contested proceedings in court).

Concerns about a child's religious upbringing may be more important to one parent than the other. Observance of religious traditions or having the children with you on special religious occasions are often of great significance to one or both parents. Sometimes one parent will want the children educated in a certain way, while the other is not even slightly concerned (unless it involves expensive school fees). Holiday arrangements – especially when there are work commitments – are also a matter of concern when considering potential arrangements. All of these issues need to be carefully thought through and negotiated.

Step children

With people changing partners more readily than they did in the 1970s, there are many more step children these days.

A step parent does not, in the absence of a court order saying otherwise, have a legal responsibility for a step child.

Step parents have no legal responsibility to pay child support.

The relationship between step parents and a step child may be very relevant in considering what arrangements are in a child's best interests.

Parents pursue their own lives

What is in the best interests of any particular child is very much open to personal interpretation. For example, having the kids sitting in a car outside the pub while a parent is inside drinking with mates may not be considered to be in their best interests. However, taking the children to visit friends who your ex does not think are desirable may well be another matter. One party's opinion of the other's friends and associates does not mean that the visit is not in the best interests of the children – unless there is a likelihood of inappropriate behaviour in front of the children, such as drug use, excessive drinking or violence.

You may not like your former partner taking the children to, say, a Pentecostal Church or an ashram. However, that is only your view. If this has been your ex-partner's faith before the separation, could you demonstrate to a court that this is now inappropriate or damaging to the children?

Usually the court is not particularly concerned about the company you keep, the religious views you follow or what sports and entertainment excite you – unless it has an adverse impact on the children and is considered to be against their welfare or their best interests.

DOES A PERSON'S BEHAVIOUR IMPACT ON THEIR ABILITY TO BE A GOOD PARENT?

In one case, the father, a respected member of the medical community, enjoyed attending gay bars dressed as a female. In negotiations over the future of their two small children, the mother stated that, unless all of her demands for the children were met (as well as her demands over a property distribution), she would reveal his behaviour to family and friends. She threatened that this would destroy his professional career.

The children knew nothing about their father's behaviour, which only took place after they went to bed. The likely impact of this behaviour on his children was, therefore, negligible.

In these circumstances, and provided the husband agreed not to engage in these practices while the children were with him, or unless they were appropriately supervised:

a) the Family Court would show little interest in her revelation, and
b) his reputation would remain intact because Family Court proceedings are entirely confidential.

The days of sensational stories about 'abnormal' behaviour being splashed across the front page of the papers have long since ended – killed 'stone dead' by the Family Law Act.

> *The Family Court has allowed children to spend time with parents who are in prison, convicted of serious crimes, drug or alcohol affected or mentally ill patients – as long as it is in safe surroundings and in the children's best interests.*
> *It's not all that long ago that some parents tried to prevent contact with another parent simply because they were gay or lesbian. How our society's values have changed!*

What happens when children's matters go to court?

It is very clear that children have rights under family law. Parents do not have similar rights but they have plenty of responsibilities. When you take a case involving children to the Family Court, your primary aim must be to ensure that your children's rights are protected.

If you are planning to fight over your children in the Family Court, stop and think, "Why am I doing this? What do I stand to achieve?" Perhaps you will decide that it is time to discuss it with your ex and negotiate a solution.

However, if children's matters end up in court, you should be aware of what happens when they do.

Pre-action process

Before you can start proceedings, you must get a certificate indicating that you have undertaken 'appropriate mediation' or 'primary dispute resolution'. This is compulsory in children's matters. It involves going to a Family Relationships Centre or an accredited Family Dispute Resolution Practitioner and attempting to resolve the issues. Hopefully this brings about agreement and you can then take a shortcut in the court process by having the agreement made legally binding through court consent orders.

However, you can still get the certificate even if you have not resolved anything at the session. Also, if one party fails to attend the session, the certificate can still be issued stating this fact.

FAMILY RELATIONSHIP CENTRES

In 2006, when the government was overhauling the family law system, it introduced Family Relationship Centres (FRCs) and a Family Advice Telephone Line.

www.familyrelationships.gov.au

or Freecall 1800 050 321

These government-supported dispute resolution services are easily accessible and publicly funded.

One of the requirements (except where there is violence or abuse) is that couples attend a Family Dispute Resolution Practitioner and get a certificate saying that they have tried to work through their issues and come to an arrangement about parenting without going to court (section 60I of the Act).

The FRCs provide limited legal advice but they do provide counselling services and a forum for working through difficult issues safely and calmly. There are now 65 FRCs throughout Australia.

Commencing proceedings

The issues relating to children that you can take to the court include:

▶   where and with whom the children are to live

▶   what time the children will spend with each parent, and

▶   what arrangements should be made for their education and religious upbringing, medical issues, what to do with passports, etc.

All of these issues will be decided according to the basic principles of what is in the child's best interest and what will promote the child's welfare.

What is relevant in determining the child's best interests?

According to the *Family Law Act*, the best interests of children are met by:

> ▶ ensuring that children have the benefit of both of their parents having a meaningful involvement in their lives to the maximum extent consistent with the best interest of the child

> ▶ protecting children from physical and psychological harm and being subjected to abuse

> ▶ ensuring that children receive full parenting to help them achieve their full potential, and

> ▶ ensuring that parents fulfil their duty to meet their responsibilities concerning the care, welfare and development of their children.

These are all great concepts and few people would argue against them. Unfortunately, each is open to interpretation, which is why many disputes over children end up in court.

Under the *Family Law Act*, the court takes into consideration a wide range of factors in determining what is in a child's best interests, including:

> ▶ the views expressed by the child

> ▶ the child's maturity and level of understanding

> ▶ the willingness and ability of each of the child's parents to facilitate and encourage a close and continuing relationship between the child and the other parent

> ▶ the practical difficulty and expense of the child spending time with, and communicating with, each parent,

> ▶ the maturity, sex, lifestyle and background – including cultural traditions of the child and of the child's parents, and

> ▶ any other factors or circumstances that the court thinks are relevant.

In other words, the court may take virtually anything into consideration in determining what is in the best interests of each child.

Although the court may "take into consideration the views of the child", children are not allowed to give evidence in court (nor, indeed, to watch events unfolding in the court). A judge has the power to interview a child but this is very rare;

children's wishes are usually determined by experts appointed by the court (see the section on child experts that follow).

Attempting to influence the children

The courts take a very dim view of a parent who tries to influence children against the other parent. Sometimes a judge will order that parents do not discuss any issues or belittle each other in the presence of the children.

You may hold genuine views about the behaviour of the other parent of your children, but trying to influence the kids to your cause is unlikely to help and will possibly have the opposite effect. So, focus on what is relevant – the children's interests. Getting this resolved will help everyone to move on.

Child experts

In many cases, child experts are appointed by the court to prepare a report on proposed arrangements for the children. Their report is provided to the court to assist in its consideration of the orders it will make.

The court will provide the expert with 'terms of reference' for the report, which might require:

> ▶ interviewing the child in the presence of the parents (first with one and then the other)

> ▶ interviewing the parents separately, and

> ▶ interviewing the child without either parent being present (depending on the age of the child).

The experts will usually assess each of the relevant factors set out in the *Family Law Act* (particularly in relation to the child's wishes and the likely impact of each of the parents' proposals on the welfare of the child) and report what they consider to be in the best interests of the child or children.

If a case proceeds to trial, the expert's report will form part of the evidence to be considered by the judge and the expert can be cross-examined on the contents of the report. An expert's opinions carry considerable weight and it is often difficult to persuade a court that the expert's recommendations should not be followed.

Independent Children's Lawyer (ICL)

At times, particularly in cases with high levels of conflict, an independent lawyer will be appointed to represent the child's best interests (but not necessarily the child's wishes). The ICL will ensure that the child's interests are presented properly to the court and will sometimes commission independent reports. This lawyer is a full participant in all of the proceedings, sitting between the lawyers for the sparring parents and/or others who are involved in the proceedings.

Judge management of children's cases

Judge management is a process in place in many of the Family Courts, designed specifically for dealing with children's issues. A judge is involved from the very early stages and everything that is said at all hearings in court is considered to be evidence in the case. The same judge will stay involved in a case from beginning to end, giving that judge the opportunity to assess the parties throughout and to be aware of everything that happens while the case is before the court.

When it's resolved – complying with court orders

Whether you and your ex agree on the arrangements for the kids, or whether the court orders have come about through the court process, once orders have been made you must comply with them – unless there are exceptional circumstances.

Exceptional circumstances might exist where you have a genuine fear that complying with orders (for example, by delivering the children to the other parent) would be placing the children in danger. If the particular danger had not been contemplated in previous court proceedings, you might be justified in withholding the children and disobeying an order. However, if your concern is that the other parent is simply an unsuitable person, or you simply don't like the terms of orders that have been made, you are not justified in deciding that the children should not go.

Relocation

Today in Australia, there is far greater social mobility than at any other time in the past. Thousands are on the move between cities and even across state borders. Some move overseas. When couples with children split up, making decisions or arrangements for their children can be compounded by the fact that the parents may also end up separated by significant distances – limiting opportunities for regular contact with their children.

Sometimes when a relationship breaks down, one of the parents may want to move to more familiar home territory, or move interstate for work or a better lifestyle.

If you want to move away from where you live and you want to take the children with you, in family law terms this is called 'relocation'. Relocation issues may arise whether or not orders are already in place.

When people want to relocate with children, the dispute often ends up in the Family Courts. Judges are then faced with the most difficult of dilemmas – to allow or to prohibit relocation. In these situations there is usually no middle ground or compromise. It becomes a decision to allow relocation (and the relocating parent takes the children away with them) or to refuse permission (and the relocating parent goes without the children or does not go at all).

RELOCATION – AN IMPOSSIBLE CHOICE

To Israel – without dad

In one case, a separated couple had very few assets and the mother wanted to relocate to Israel, from where the couple had migrated 10 years earlier. She had little support and few friends in Australia and her parents and social support system were in Israel. In contrast, the father had a stable and well-paid job in Australia and had many friends and family support.

The Family Court considered that both were excellent parents to their three children, aged four, six and nine and were well loved by each of them. Despite their separation, both parents participated actively in the children's lives and were flexible in arrangements around where the children spent time.

The mother brought an application in the Family Court seeking to relocate to Israel with the three children. Not surprisingly, the father objected to the application, especially as the family's finances would prevent him from travelling to Israel or bringing the children to Australia for holidays.

In what must have been an impossibly difficult decision, the court allowed the mother to return to Israel, concluding that it was in the children's best interests that they return with her. The decision was a disaster for the father but, with the parties unable to agree, the court had to make a decision on the basis of considerations of the children's welfare – despite the distressing consequences.
Sadly, relocation cases are often like this.

In Mount Isa – without mum

A couple moved to Mt Isa with their young children to enable the father to pursue his career in the mining industry. The marriage broke down and the mother wished to return with the children to Sydney where the parties had previously lived.

The matter went to the High Court of Australia which confirmed the Family Court's decision that it was not in the best interests of the children to be removed from Mt Isa.

Ironically, after the case was decided – after years of argument and tens of thousands of dollars in legal expenses – the mother formed a relationship in Mt Isa and decided to stay ... and the father has since moved elsewhere.

Life is complex and the decisions the court is asked to make are often gut wrenching.

Abduction – taking the law into your own hands

Sometimes, the arrangements specified by the court for a child to spend time with a parent are strongly opposed by the other parent. But even if you disapprove of the court's decision and think it's completely wrong, don't try to remove the child from the country unless you have the approval of the court.

Attempting to flee overseas with the child or children is not recommended because:

▸ The other parent can arrange to have your name and/or the child's name placed on a Federal Police watch list, maintained at every international port and airport in Australia. Once listed, you will be unable to leave Australia.

▸ It would be contrary to an order of the Family Court and the court does not take kindly to a party who breaches an order.

▸ The child or children may be ordered to be returned to Australia (at your expense) under an international Child Abduction Convention (the Hague Convention), an international agreement that applies in over 85 countries including Australia.

Taking children out of Australia

Taking children out of Australia in contravention of a court order is abduction. The consequences of this can be extremely severe and you are likely to be compelled to bring the children back to Australia and face court action.

If you do nothing else, make sure you get proper legal advice about your responsibilities. The abduction laws are administered by the Federal Attorney General's Department (although any court action in Australia will still take place in the Family Courts).

CHILD ABDUCTION

Attorney General's Department
1800 100 480 or email CentralAuthority@ag.gov.au.
www.ema.gov.au/www/agd/agd.nsf/Page/Families_Children_
Internationalchildabduction

If you find that your children have been abducted and taken outside Australia, get legal advice and/or advise the Commonwealth Attorney General's Department immediately to try to have them returned. If you're lucky, the children will have been taken to a country that is covered by the Hague Convention. Many countries are parties to this convention (including most of Europe and the United States) and the return of the children is likely to be enforced.

Beware – some of our nearest neighbours (including Malaysia, Indonesia and most Asian countries) are not parties to the convention and recovery of children from those countries may not be possible.

Passports

Children's passports are often an issue. Under Australian law, both parents must sign an application for a child's passport. The child cannot travel internationally without a passport. Where one has already been issued, the parent holding the passport may travel with the child. So it's a powerful issue.

Where a passport is sought, a parent can approach the court and ask for orders compelling the other parent to sign the application and, in extreme circumstances, for the court to sign on behalf of a refusing parent.

Where there are concerns about the possible use of a child's passport, you can request the court to hold a passport until further orders that might permit its use.

If a child has dual nationality, but no passport has yet been issued, it may be helpful to notify the embassy or consular representatives of the other country and request that no new passport be issued. However, this is not a watertight solution and may not be as effective as steps you might take in Australia, such as placing children on the Federal Watch List or obtaining orders that all passports be held by the Family Court (possibly including the other parent's passport).

Child abuse and violence

Our society does not condone the abuse of anyone, let alone children. Abuse has extremely serious effects on a child and significant implications in law.

Abuse takes many forms and should be reported promptly so it can be investigated by the appropriate authorities. There are obligations under federal and state laws for the compulsory reporting of suspected or actual child abuse.

What is abuse?

Child abuse is harm to, or neglect of, a child by another person, whether adult or child. It can be physical, verbal, sexual or through neglect.

▸ Physical abuse sometimes results in serious injury to the child and is often evident though welts, bruises or burns.

▸ Verbal abuse often results in aggressive or withdrawn behaviour and a child that is afraid to go home.

▸ Sexual abuse can be recognised by a range of physical, emotional and behavioural signs.

> ▸ Neglect can be seen in the child being unwashed or uncared for, undernourished or in obvious need of medical or dental treatment.

The type of abuse is essentially irrelevant under the law. If abuse occurs, or if you have reasonable grounds to believe that there is abuse, take any evidence you have to the police or to the child welfare authorities in your state. If you have a lawyer, also advise him or her about your concerns or any action that you may have taken.

However, making false claims may well rebound on you. Not only is it against the law but such claims throw serious doubt on your credibility.

TO REPORT SUSPECTED CHILD ABUSE

Australian Capital Territory   1300 556 729
www.dhcs.act.gov.au/ocyfs/care_protection.htm

NSW   13 21 11
www.community.nsw.gov.au

Northern Territory   1800 700 250
www.health.nt.gov.au/health/comm_svs/facs/child_protect/child_protect.
shtml

Queensland   1800 811 810
www.childsafety.qld.gov.au

South Australia   13 14 78
www.familiesandcommunities.sa.gov.au

Tasmania 1300 737 639
www.dhhs.tas.gov.au

Victoria   13 12 78
www.dhs.vic.gov.au/childprotection

Western Australia   1800 199 008
www.community.wa.gov

DO'S & DON'TS

A prominent child psychologist provided the following list of what to do and what not to do for separated parents:

1. *Talk to your children about your separation*

Talk to your kids. Tell them, in very simple terms, what it all means to them and their lives. When parents do not explain what's happening to their children, kids feel anxious, upset and lonely and find it much harder to cope with the separation.

2. *Be discreet*

Reorganise things in a way that respects your children's relationship with both parents. Don't leave letters or court papers out on your kitchen counter for children to read. Don't talk to your best friend, your mother or your lawyer about legal matters or your ex when the kids can hear you. Kids are ill-equipped to understand these adult matters.

3. *Act like grown-ups: keep your conflict away from the kids*

No one stands to benefit by involving the children in your disputes – doing so ends up hurting everyone.

4. *Stay in the picture*

The more involved parents are after separation and divorce, the better for the children. Where a good parent-child relationship exists, kids grow through adolescence just as well adjusted as married-family children. Develop a child-centred parenting plan that allows a continuing and meaningful relationship with both parents. High levels of appropriate parental involvement are linked to better academic functioning in kids as well as better adjustment overall. Help with homework and projects, use appropriate discipline and be emotionally available to talk about problems.

5. *Deal with anger appropriately*

In their anger and pain, one parent may actively try to keep the other out of the children's lives – even when they are a good parent who the children love. When you're hurting, it's easy to think you never want to see the 'ex' again and to convince yourself that's also best for the kids but children's needs during separation are very different from their parents.

6.   Be a good parent

Going through a separation is not a holiday from parenting – providing appropriate discipline, monitoring your children, maintaining your expectations about school, being emotionally available. Competent parenting has emerged as one of the most important protective factors in terms of children's positive adjustment to separation.

7.   Manage your own mental health

Seek help if feelings of depression, anxiety or anger continue to overwhelm you. Even a few sessions of therapy can be enormously useful. Remember, your own mental health has an impact on your children.

8.   Keep the people your children care about in their lives

Encourage your children to stay connected to your ex's family and important friends. If possible, use the same babysitters or child care. This stable network strengthens a child's feeling that they are not alone in this world but have a deep and powerful support system – an important factor in becoming a psychologically healthy adult.

9.   Be thoughtful about your future love life

Take time, a lot of time, before you remarry or cohabit again. Ask yourself: must your children meet everyone you date? Young children, in particular, form attachments to your potential life partners and if new relationships break up, loss after loss may lead to depression and lack of trust in children. Don't expect your older kids to instantly love someone you've chosen – this person will have to earn their respect and affection.

10.   Pay your child support

Pay child support regularly – even if you're angry or access to your children is withheld. Children whose parents separate or divorce face much more economic instability than their married counterparts, even when support is paid. Don't make the situation worse. Let your message to the kids be that you care so much about them that you will keep them separate and safe, from any conflict. They will appreciate it as they get older.

CHILDREN'S ISSUES – RESOURCES

▶ *A very useful website providing information and direction regarding children's matters is the Australian Government Attorney-General's Department:*
www.ag.gov.au

▶ *Go to 'Family Relationships Online' under the topic 'Families and marriage'.*

DIVIDING UP THE PROPERTY – IT'S AS SIMPLE AS 1, 2, 3

SUMMARY

▶ Property matters in family law are the issues involved in the division of your assets and liabilities after separation. They are also referred to as financial matters.

▶ Under family law, 'property' includes many things – it is not just cash and houses. If you have a family business, a trust, investments, an entitlement to be paid, superannuation or even a pension entitlement, it is likely to be defined as property.

▶ Property also includes money you owe and any other liabilities of the relationship.

▶ All property will be included for consideration in the financial distribution after separation.

▶ Make sure you divide your property legally. You might divide property by informal agreement, but if you don't do this according to the *Family Law Act* and your ex later wants another slice of the property, you could be in for a nasty surprise.

▶ It's not just about what you own and owe; it's about what you've contributed. The roles you had during your relationship and who has made what contributions are factors that will be considered when dividing up your property.

▶ What each of you is likely to need in the future will also be taken into account.

▶ You will not receive less in a property distribution simply because you personally brought in fewer dollars during the relationship or because you were a homemaker.

- It is very important that you tell the truth about what you own, to each other and to the court. This is called 'full and frank disclosure'. If you don't, you could end up transferring a lot more to your ex than you thought you might save by not disclosing all the information.

- Don't go off and spend money or destroy property to try to minimise the amount your ex will get. This is likely to backfire and may be deducted from the property you receive in the distribution.

- Superannuation is included in property distribution, but is not necessarily treated the same way as other property.

What is property?

When a couple separates, they will have to decide how their property will be divided between them (and how to split up the debts).

The definition of 'property' for family law purposes is:

> *"property to which parties (to a marriage or de facto relationship) are, or that party is, as the case may be, entitled, whether in possession or reversion."*

This definition may not seem to be very helpful but, in everyday language, for family law purposes property means virtually anything – whether it is an asset or a liability (debt of some kind).

Property does not just include real estate (homes, farms, apartments, office blocks, vacant land). It may also include:

- personal items (furniture, kitchenware, white goods)

- money (cash, bank accounts)

- debts owed to you or by you (to the bank as mortgages or personal loans, credit cards, loans from, or to, friends or business associates)

- investments (shares, interests in a business or company, timeshares)

- a family business

- a trust

- ▶ an entitlement to be paid or a liability to pay in the event that something happens

- ▶ intellectual property

- ▶ lottery winnings, and

- ▶ gifts from parents and relatives and, in some circumstances, inheritances.

Property even includes entitlements to redundancy or long-service payments, leave entitlements, pensions and superannuation.

Whatever you can think of, it is almost certainly 'property' in the family law sense.

And that means **all of the property** – whether it's in your name, your partner's name, joint names, a company name you may have an interest in, or even property in someone else's name that you have some entitlement to. In effect:

> *What's yours is ours, what's mine is ours and what's ours is ours.*

It's all in the pot and available for distribution between you, even if one party has never shown any interest in it, did not want it and tried to get rid of it. If it's still there, it's included in the pot. And if it's not property, it will usually be regarded as a 'financial resource' (see Glossary of Terms on page 209).

Sometimes, especially in a short relationship, dividing up the property can be pretty easy as there is not much to split between you. In these cases, you probably would not worry about getting a formal agreement drafted up and registered in the courts (but beware, this may come back to bite you, as the cautionary tale that follows on page 56 'Losing the lottery after you have won it' demonstrates).

It can get to be quite complicated where a lot of property has been accumulated over the years or where there are complex financial arrangements and structures. This is when you almost certainly need some good legal advice and a formal agreement.

Whether easy or complicated, always remember that the arrangements you make with your ex-partner will not be legally binding (that is, you cannot make the other party abide by the agreement) unless registered in the courts as consent orders or prepared, according to the law, as a Financial Agreement.

You can settle your property distribution by mutual agreement or you can go to court to ask for a decision from a judge. The principles that should guide you in arriving at a private settlement and the law that the court will apply are the same. Just follow the 'Three steps of property distribution' on page 57 in this chapter.

LOSING THE LOTTERY AFTER YOU HAVE WON IT

When they split, a married couple had very little property, made no agreement and just went their separate ways. Their one child stayed with the wife and the husband had little to do with either of them in the following years (and didn't provide much financial support either).

Neither party bothered to apply for a divorce so they remained legally married. Therefore, each of them retained the right to commence proceedings for a property distribution (a right that continues for 12 months after a divorce).

In a stroke of fortune, the husband won first prize of $5 million in a state lottery. The wife brought a claim in the Family Court for a share of the winnings.

The court decided that she had a right to a share of the lottery winnings. It said that the money was part of the 'property' of the parties and its value was "to be determined at the date of the determination, not the date of separation or some other time."

The court awarded the wife $1.5 million of the $5 million the husband had won. Moral of the story – if you want certainty, finalise arrangements by a properly executed legal agreement.

Time limits

There are a couple of statutory limitations (legal time limits), to be careful of in family law. A statutory limitation prevents you starting proceedings in court after a certain period of time. If you don't commence your action before the time limit expires, you lose the automatic right to get the issues into court.

It's not always an absolute disaster if you miss a statutory deadline as, under family law, you can still apply to the court for special permission to commence your action 'out of time'. However, this approach is not recommended – the court might simply say "no" and that would be the end of that.

The following time limits are important:

▶ You may apply for a divorce after you have been separated for 12 months.

▶ For up to 12 months after a divorce has been granted, you may apply to the Family Courts for orders in relation to property settlement. After that time, you will have to get the court's permission to start any application involving property matters (which include spousal maintenance or financial support issues).

▶ If you are in a de facto relationship, you can bring an application to the Family Court for property matters up to 24 months after your separation. If you do not apply within this time, you will have to seek the court's permission to start proceedings.

The three steps of property distribution

Lawyers are often criticised for complicating the law and making it almost impossible to understand. We are going to do the opposite – even at the risk of being accused of being simplistic – and explain the principles of property or financial distribution in a very straight-forward way.

You only have to answer three questions to decide who is entitled to what property:

1. What are the assets and liabilities, and what is their value?

2. Who made what contribution to those assets and liabilities (before, during and after the relationship)?

3. Are there any factors that would support an adjustment of the allocation of property in favour of one person or the other?

Although some lawyers may make the process seem far more complicated, this is how it works.

In Step 1, you determine the net pool available for distribution, which will be expressed as a dollar figure.

The processes in Steps 2 and 3 are usually expressed as percentages of the net pool from the Step 1 assessment, for example, a 10 per cent additional contribution (Step 2) or a 5 per cent adjustment (Step 3).

The steps in more detail, are as follows:

Step 1 – Assess the assets and liabilities

Every item of property has a value and, if in doubt, there is always someone who will be able to provide a professional valuation. This could be a real estate agent, a motor vehicle dealer, a jewellery valuer, a business expert, etc.

Family law is interested only in the monetary value of property. Sentimental value is not relevant (although it may be material to how you personally 'value' a particular item of property). You may regard Granny's necklace as priceless but an expert will put a dollar value on it. A value can also be made for any business or investment and for superannuation or pensions.

Holiday pay, redundancy and long-service leave entitlements also have a value and go into the asset pool. Even life insurance policies and wills are sometimes included. You may need an accountant to help you with this.

ASSET AND LIABILITY CALCULATIONS

A good way to tackle negotiations for financial distribution is to prepare a spreadsheet that includes all of the assets and liabilities.

This gives you a good picture of where you stand and also identifies what assets and liabilities have to be included in any agreement or orders (if you leave something out you may end up in court to tie up the loose ends).

A schedule like this also enables you to work out the percentage distribution of how much of the assets you will get.

Put the assets and liabilities into columns and see what each totals. Then take the total liabilities away from the total assets. The result is the net value of the asset pool.

In the example that follows, we have set out the assets at the top (total $1,000,000) and the liabilities underneath (total $300,000). Subtract the liabilities from the assets to get the net asset figure ($700,000).

Then add in the superannuation ($300,000) to arrive at the total asset figure of $1,000,000 (we will explain later why it is best to total superannuation separately). We have also included a column showing who owns each item of property – as 'mine' and 'yours'. This will help when you have to work out transfers of property that might have to take place.

	Owner	Value
Assets		
Real Estate		
Home	Joint	$500,000
Investment Property	Joint	$300,000
Personal Property		
Furniture	Joint	$35,000
Other	Yours	$15,000
Motor vehicles		
Car 1	Mine	$30,000
Car 2	Yours	$20,000
Other Assets		
1	Mine	$25,000
2	Yours	$25,000
3	Joint	$50,000
Total Assets		**$1,000,000**
Liabilities		
Mortgages		
Home	Joint	$150,000
Investment Property	Mine	$100,000
Personal Loans		
Car	Mine	$20,000
Whitegoods	Joint	$10,000
Credit Cards		
Card 1	Mine	$15,000
Card 2	Yours	$5,000
Total Liabilities		**$300,000**
Net Assets		**$700,000**
Superannuation		
ABC Fund	Mine	$200,000
XYZ Fund	Mine	$50,000
XYZ Fund	Yours	$50,000
Total Superannuation		**$300,000**
Total Assets		**$1,000,000**

When do you value the assets and liabilities?

The value of your assets and liabilities will be made at the date the property is divided between you.

If the matter goes to court, the value will be what things are worth at the time of the trial.

If you are settling matters between yourselves, there is more flexibility as to the value. You may agree the values between yourselves, but they should still reflect approximate values at the date of your agreement.

How do you value the property?

If you cannot agree on values and are going to court, experts will have to be engaged. This can be a costly exercise, especially if you have businesses to value. Even valuations of homes may involve registered valuers. These costs are significant. An argument over jewellery, antiques and other valuables might also involve professional valuers. Other professionals can value your furniture and household effects.

The alternative – and a very much cheaper one – is to agree on values wherever you can.

Obtain several appraisals from real estate agents for your properties (these are free) and agree to take an average of, say, three appraisals. Get your accountant to place a value on your business interests and see if you can agree on that too. Try splitting your personal effects and furniture by mutual agreement. There are several ways of achieving a fair split without getting expensive valuations done. Compromise is the key.

In some cases, it will not be possible to agree on values, especially where the stakes are high and the consequences of the distribution may be unfair to one party – for example, where the separating couple own a business that one of them will keep after the distribution of property. The business may have provided the sole source of income for the parties during their relationship and, therefore, its value will be very important for the party who is not keeping that interest. A professional valuation by an agreed valuer may be the only way to produce a fair result and, in such cases, the parties will simply have to wear the costs and move on – ideally as quickly as possible, as protracted arguments over values are rarely of benefit to anyone but the professionals who charge fees for preparing the valuation reports.

Beware of values that may be volatile or change quickly, such as the price of shares and other financial investments. Make sure that the value you are agreeing to is the value at the date of implementation of your agreement, or you may find yourself short-changed.

The value you place on bank accounts and credit cards is also a potential trap. Make sure you are very clear about what is included and what is not. For example:

▶ Is a tax refund coming in soon? How much is it likely to be and who is entitled to it?

▶ Is one party cranking up a credit card that the other has to pay?

Just make sure the rules are agreed between you, as this leaves far less possibility for argument down the track.

WHAT IS IT WORTH?

The task of valuing assets can often be simple – but this is not always the case.

The family home and real estate
Often it will be sufficient to obtain a written opinion of value from a local estate agent (an appraisal) at no cost.

However, where there is no agreement about the real value, it will be necessary to engage a professional valuer to conduct an inspection and write a report. This is usually done on behalf of both parties and, in most cases, the parties will share the cost of the report equally. The cost will depend on the size, nature and value of the property and is generally between $800 and $1,500.

Vehicles
In most cases, it will be enough to provide an estimate of value, or an internet print out from a car sales website such as the RedBook (www.redbook.com.au). Vintage and luxury cars are an exception. Remember to make an allowance for any loans taken out to purchase the car.

Furniture, artwork and jewellery

Furniture and other belongings are often not valued because, in most cases, the resale value is extremely low. Second-hand auction value is the standard for personal property in family law, which is always very low and only a fraction of replacement value.

The most common approach is to estimate the value of this property or to disregard it altogether.

If furniture and belongings are an important part of your settlement, we would suggest preparing a list of items you would like to keep so that these matters can be raised and agreed early in the negotiations.

Of course, if there are expensive items, such as artwork or antique furniture, it may be worthwhile to have these items valued.

Jewellery is not always valued unless there are especially valuable pieces and will usually be kept by the person in possession. Generally, engagement and wedding rings will not form part of a property pool and will be kept by the wearer.

Companies, businesses and trusts

Valuing companies, business and trust assets can be a difficult task and experts will often have to be engaged to provide a valuation.

If it is clear that a business or a company is not very profitable, it may not be cost effective to obtain a valuation. Often it will be enough to rely on the financial documents and an accountant's report.

The valuation of these types of assets or resources requires ongoing co-operation by both parties. If you are not willing to co-operate, it can be expensive to obtain a valuation or to identify whether the company or business is even profitable.

Step 2 – Assess the contributions

Having worked out what is in the pool of assets and placed a value on each asset and debt, family law requires that the parties' respective contributions be assessed.

Under the *Family Law Act*, there are three different types of contribution:

- ▶ **Financial contributions (direct and indirect).** These contributions include the incomes of the parties during the relationship, property that was owned by one party at the start of the relationship (or received during the relationship or after separation) and gifts or inheritances received during the relationship. Windfalls during the relationship, such as a lottery win, will probably be a joint contribution – no matter who bought the ticket.

- ▶ **Non-financial contributions.** These are contributions that are not measured directly in dollar terms ('contributions in kind'), for example, if one of you worked nights and weekends on an investment property to help increase its value, or one supported the other by attending business functions and provided general assistance to enable them to carry on a business.

- ▶ **Contributions to the welfare of the family.** This includes looking after the children and domestic duties generally, for example, washing and ironing, cleaning and shopping. In family law, welfare contributions are not treated as inferior to financial contributions.

At the end of this step, it is usual to express each party's contributions in percentage terms, such as a 60 per cent contribution (as opposed to a 40 per cent contribution by the other person). In this situation, one person's contributions have been assessed as 10 per cent greater than the other, resulting in a 60 per cent (contribution-based) entitlement to the overall asset pool and leaving 40 per cent to the other person.

A note about the percentages

In most family law cases that go to court, the distribution of property is determined by using a percentage assessment of each party's total entitlement, for example 60/40 or 50/50 on a global basis (that is, looking at the total of the asset pool).

In a very limited number of cases, the court assesses contributions by using what is called an 'asset-by-asset' approach, where the contribution of a party to a specific item of property is taken into account (for example, one party may have made the overwhelming contribution to a house inherited from their parent).

Whatever the percentage distribution is, family law requires that it be fair and reasonable.

Contributions prior to the relationship

Contributions to the asset pool are not restricted to what happened during the relationship. A contribution will also be taken into account if it was made prior to when the relationship began or after the couple separated.

Contributions made prior to the relationship can be important, especially in shorter relationships. For example, if the asset pool in a five-year relationship is $500,000 and $300,000 was brought in by one party at the beginning, that person will have made a substantially greater contribution to the property pool. This would then entitle them to a greater share of the asset pool when it is divided up. It is not simply a case of giving them back what they brought in.

Post-separation contributions

Contributions can also be made after separation. This is most common when one party is:

- ▸ looking after the children (and therefore making a welfare contribution)

- ▸ paying the mortgage and maintaining the home after separation (and therefore making direct and indirect financial contributions), or

- ▸ when improvements have been made to an asset by one party after separation but before the date the distribution is determined.

Post-separation contributions do not generally carry a lot of weight, unless they are very substantial (such as an inheritance or a gift received after separation) or there has been a long period of time between separation and the property settlement.

Step 3 – Assess any further adjustments: the 'Section 75(2) factors'

The third step in the property process is to look at other things that might justify one person receiving a further adjustment to give them a greater share of the available asset pool.

The factors justifying an adjustment are set out in Section 75(2) of the *Family Law Act*. They take into account each partner's situation and include the following:

- ▶ both parties' age and health

- ▶ income-earning capacity

- ▶ any responsibilities that you or your ex-partner may have for children of the relationship (after the separation)

- ▶ financial resources

- ▶ what might be a reasonable standard of living in the circumstances after separation

- ▶ the financial circumstances one of you may be in if you are in another relationship

- ▶ how long you lived together, and

- ▶ whether child support is being paid.

It also includes:

> *"any fact or circumstance which, in the opinion of the court, the justice of the case requires to be taken into account."*

In simple language, this last factor means that the law permits a judge to take into account virtually anything. In practice, however, the courts have been quite restrictive about what they are prepared to take into account. For example, they do not consider a party's moral behaviour to be material to the financial outcome.

Violence by one party against another is generally regarded as relevant to financial distribution only if the violence has an impact on the other person's contributions, for example, by making it difficult for a party to carry out domestic tasks.

Examples of factors that may be considered relevant include:

▸ If you have been at home looking after the children for many years and you have little prospect of getting a properly paid job (here a financial adjustment would probably be made to offset the fact that you may struggle to re-enter the workforce and have no capacity to support yourself as a result of your responsibilities for the children during, and after, the relationship).

▸ If one of you is elderly (beyond working age) and/or has health problems, while the other is in good health (and, therefore, has a greater capacity to work and support themselves), an adjustment may be made in favour of the less able person.

▸ If you have not worked for some time but intend to undertake a training course or studies that would help you to re-enter the workforce, an adjustment might be made (or spousal maintenance paid) to assist in this regard.

▸ If you are still responsible for the care and welfare of your children and you wish to continue that role, it may be necessary for an adjustment to be made to support that.

At the end of the day, each case will depend entirely on its own facts and it would be wise to get legal advice about how adjustments might work in your particular situation.

Length of the relationship

How long parties have lived together is important. The longer you have been together, the more likely it is that your assets will be more equally shared after separation (and the less important the initial contributions will be considered, even if they were substantial).

The length of a relationship is taken from the time the parties start living together in a domestic relationship ('co-habitation'). If you are married, the beginning of your relationship will not necessarily be the date of your marriage; it will start when you began to live together. This can be a significant factor when parties have lived together for a long time before getting married. The whole of their time together is taken into consideration to assess the length of the relationship (and determine whether one party might be entitled to an adjustment as a result).

A possible fourth step – who keeps what?

A fourth step may be appropriate but it's not one you will find in the *Family Law Act*. That step is to work out who ends up with each asset and liability.

For example:

- Who will keep the Holden and who gets the Ford?

- Who will have the home transferred to them and be responsible for the mortgage payments?

- After the other property has been split up, what cash adjustment needs to be made to get the percentages right?

This requires you to assess which proposals are realistic and which are simply not possible. For example, it is pointless agreeing that one partner will keep the house and the mortgage if that person is unable to meet the mortgage payments from their income.

A word about spousal maintenance

'Spousal maintenance' is financial support one party provides to the other after the relationship has ended (whether married or de facto). Spousal maintenance is part of the property section of the *Family Law Act* and the time limits discussed earlier will apply.

Generally, spousal maintenance is payable where:

- one party has a need for financial support

- the other party has the capacity to provide that support, and

- it would be proper in all the circumstances that the support be provided.

Typically, this would occur where one person is the income earner and the other has inadequate means of support as a consequence of the separation. Ongoing income payments may be required if there are insufficient assets to distribute, which would give the needy party some other means of support.

Maintenance may be payable for a short period of time or may be payable indefinitely.

Spousal maintenance can be paid under a court order or by agreement between the parties.

Sometimes spousal maintenance is included in a property settlement, by way of a lump sum, or as an allowance of the percentage distribution, as a substitute for ongoing regular payments. This can be done by nominating the lump sum amount in a settlement and/or in orders or by adjusting the percentage distribution.

You should seek legal advice if you are on either side of the spousal maintenance equation. This will give you some pointers about entitlements or obligations and about the proper way to give legal effect to lump sum payments.

Family law – a discretionary jurisdiction

Remember, family law is discretionary and judges have a broad range within which they make their final decisions. No one can predict exactly what the result will be. Lawyers can only give you a range within which the matter is likely to be decided – something like "you will receive somewhere between 45 and 55 per cent of the net assets". So, if you launch into Family Court proceedings to resolve your property dispute, make sure that what you are seeking is well within the probable range.

HOW SIMPLE IS IT TO ASSESS A PROPERTY DISTRIBUTION?

A survey carried out by a university law school some years ago compared the assessments of around 500 experienced family lawyers (including judges and magistrates) of what they believed was a 'fair and reasonable' distribution. The same scenario was given to each person.

*The assessments – which were taken at random over 10 years – **varied by more than 40 per cent.** That is a huge difference among those who are meant to know the answer!*

*Keep this in mind if you decide you want the issues decided in court or when your lawyer tells you that you will **definitely** get 60 or 70 per cent of the asset pool.*

When assessing what you might end up with from a property settlement, don't forget to take into account your possible legal fees.

You may be spending a lot of money in legal fees for the privilege of having your dispute dealt with by the courts. For example, if you are looking at a property settlement percentage difference of five per cent and your lawyer tells you that your legal fees are likely to be around $50,000, the money you spend on those fees may be more than the percentage difference you are arguing about. In other words, if you are arguing over five per cent and the legal fees might be $50,000, your total net property would have to be worth well over $1 million to make the argument worthwhile.

Always make this calculation in your decision-making process, whether the legal fees are fixed by your lawyer or are estimates of what it might cost (in which case, take the top end of the estimate).

The benefits of trying to get matters resolved by agreement and staying out of the courts – and the value of compromise – are obvious.

An example of the property distribution process

The following hypothetical scenario illustrates how the property distribution process described might work in practice.

Mick and Michelle have decided to separate. They are both in their mid 40s, have been married for 10 years (but living together for 15) and have two children aged 11 and 13. Mick works full time and earns $75,000 a year. The kids are at school and Michelle works part time, earning $20,000.

Mick's parents gave him $100,000 towards the purchase of a $350,000 home ten years ago. The house is now worth $500,000, but Mick and Michelle still have a mortgage of $150,000.

Their other assets are two cars valued at $25,000 (Mick's) and $10,000 (Michelle's), some personal property (furniture and personal effects) valued at $15,000 and Mick has a share portfolio worth $25,000, which he hoped would be an investment for the children.

There is a car loan in Mick's name with $10,000 outstanding and a consumer loan in joint names for $5,000.

Mick has a superannuation policy with his employer, with a present value of $100,000. If he remains in this job, he can expect to have super of about $500,000 by the time he retires in 15-20 years (which he can convert to a pension or take as a lump sum).

Mick and Michelle have agreed that the children will spend roughly equal amounts of time with each of them, although Mick's work commitments mean he will be unable to look after the children during school holidays.

They have agreed that child support will be paid in accordance with whatever the Child Support Agency (CSA) determines. They do not want to go to court and have asked their lawyers to work out a fair and reasonable property settlement to get the whole matter finalised.

Do the 1, 2 and 3. Put these facts into the three-step process.

Step 1 – Determine the asset and liability pool

Mick and Michelle's schedule of assets and liabilities would look like this:

Assets	
Home (Joint)	$500,000
Car (Mick)	$15,000
Car (Michelle)	$10,000
Personal property	$15,000
Share portfolio (Mick)	$25,000
Sub Total of Assets	**$565,000**
Liabilities	
Home (Joint)	$150,000
Car loan (Mick)	$10,000
Consumer loan (Joint)	$5,000
Sub Total of Liabilities	**$165,000**
Net Property (Assets less Liabilities)	**$400,000**
Superannuation (Mick)	$100,000
Total	**$500,000**

Step 2 – What are the contributions?

Mick

- ▸ made the major direct financial contribution

- ▸ made an additional substantial financial contribution through his parents' gift of $100,000, and

- ▸ made a welfare contribution through his care of the children.

Michelle

- ▸ also contributed financially with her income, and

- ▸ made the major contribution to the welfare of the family in caring for the children and looking after the domestic responsibilities.

Mick might be entitled to an additional 10-15 per cent for the money brought in from his parents, giving him 60-65 per cent of the net assets after Step 2.

Step 3 – Are there any factors warranting an adjustment?

Mick

- ▸ we assume that he will be retaining the whole of his super (which he cannot access until he retires), and

- ▸ is paying child support in accordance with the CSA assessment.

Michelle

- ▸ earns far less than Mick and this is unlikely to change

- ▸ may have more responsibilities for caring for the children, and

- ▸ is receiving child support in accordance with the assessment.

Michelle may be entitled to an adjustment of 15-20 per cent in her favour after completing Step 3 of the process.

The maths on these ranges results in 50-60 per cent to Michelle of the overall pool:

- ▸ Michelle's +15 - 20 per cent in Step 3

less

▶   Mick's +10 - 15 per cent in Step 2

equals

▶   A possible additional distribution of between 0 and 10 per cent of the total net assets for Michelle.

This means Michelle may be entitled to a distribution of between $250,000 and $300,000 of the net assets (50 - 60 per cent of $500,000).

The final distribution

Mick and Michelle agree they will settle by distributing 60 per cent of their net property to Michelle ($300,000) with a further agreement that Mick (who will receive $200,000) will not have to pay any ongoing spousal maintenance to support Michelle. A fair and reasonable distribution in these circumstances might be:

Michelle

Home & mortgage (net value)	*$500,000*
Personal effects	*$5,000*
Car	*$10,000*
	$515,000

Less

Mortgage	*$150,000*
Loan	*$5,000*
	$155,000

Total to Michelle	***$360,000***

Mick

Share portfolio	*$15,000*
Personal property	*$10,000*
Car	*$25,000*
Superannuation	*<u>$100,000</u>*
	$150,000

Less

Car loan	*$10,000*

Total to Mick	***$140,000***

Michelle is receiving $60,000 more than the agreed 60 per cent, so she has to find this money to pay Mick so he gets his agreed 40 per cent ($200,000). She may be in a position to increase the mortgage or, maybe, borrow from her parents. If she is unable to do that, they may have to re-arrange the settlement so that Mick keeps the home and pays Michelle the amount needed to bring her up to 60 per cent – or the home might have to be sold.

Another alternative might be for them to have an agreement that allows Michelle to stay in the home until the youngest child turns 18, when the house will be sold and the proceeds divided equally between them (or even in Mick's favour).

There are endless possibilities to consider in arriving at a result that works best. Don't stop searching for a solution just because the first proposal does not seem to stack up.

The couple in our example could have spent tens of thousands of dollars on legal costs, each trying to get the absolute best outcome for themselves. They would have done so without any guarantee about the result and, after deducting the legal costs from the assets, both could have been worse off. If they each spent $40,000 on legal costs (certainly a possibility if the matter went to trial), the asset pool available to divide would have been reduced by $80,000 (more than 15 per cent).

A UNIQUE WAY OF DIVIDING PROPERTY

A wealthy couple agreed to divide all their assets equally, including their many paintings.

However, hostilities broke out during negotiations, as the wife felt the husband was keeping the best art works and undervaluing them. She really wanted a valuable painting by celebrated Australian artist Clifton Pugh, and she thought the valuation obtained by her husband was too low. The painting remained in the former matrimonial home where the husband continued to live.

To 'resolve' the situation, the wife returned to the home, took the painting from the wall and broke it into two pieces – taking one half with her. She considered this to be an 'equal distribution' of the property.

Unfortunately for her, the judge did not see it that way. The fact that the artwork was effectively destroyed by the wife's actions resulted in her 'receiving' the whole of the value of the painting in the property distribution.

Disclosure of financial information

An issue that often causes problems in property matters is full and complete disclosure of all the relevant financial information.

Failure to provide adequate information is a significant reason why many cases end up going to court, rather than getting settled.

In family law, you have a duty to make a full and unqualified disclosure of your financial position to your ex-partner. This includes not just bank statements and title deeds but any information that is even remotely relevant to your financial position, including any interest in trusts, companies and also any interest or involvement in anything that is not even in your name.

The Family Courts are very strict in their interpretation of this duty.

Just so this is really clear, this is what 13.04 of the *Family Law Rules* states regarding your duty to disclose:

1) A party to a financial case must make full and frank disclosure of the party's financial circumstances, including:

   a) the party's earnings, including income that is paid or assigned to another party, person or legal entity;

   b) any vested or contingent interest in property;

   c) any vested or contingent interest in property owned by a legal entity that is fully or partially owned or controlled by a party;

   d) any income earned by a legal entity fully or partially owned or controlled by a party, including income that is paid or assigned to any other party, person or legal entity;

   e) the party's other financial resources;

   f) any trust:

      i) of which the party is the appointor or trustee;

      ii) of which the party, the party's child, spouse or de facto spouse is an eligible beneficiary as to capital or income;

      iii) of which a corporation is an eligible beneficiary as to capital or income if the party, or the party's child, spouse or de facto spouse is a shareholder or director of the corporation;

      iv) over which the party has any direct or indirect power or control;

      v) of which the party has the direct or indirect power to remove or appoint a trustee;

      vi) of which the party has the power (whether subject to the concurrence of another person or not) to amend the terms;

      vii) of which the party has the power to disapprove a proposed amendment of the terms or the appointment or removal of a trustee; or

      viii) over which a corporation has a power mentioned in any of subparagraphs (iv) to (vii), if the party, the party's child, spouse or de facto spouse is a director or shareholder of the corporation;

> g)   any disposal of property (whether by sale, transfer, assignment or gift) made by the party, a legal entity mentioned in paragraph (c), a corporation or a trust mentioned in paragraph (f) that may affect, defeat or deplete a claim:
>
> i)   in the 12 months immediately before the separation of the parties; or
>
> ii)   since the final separation of the parties; and
>
> h)   liabilities and contingent liabilities.

One of the tips we gave in chapter 1 'When it's over, it's over' is that you should copy (or scan) as many financial documents as possible before you or the other party leaves home. If your partner does not 'play ball' and give a full disclosure of documents they may control (for example, bank accounts, investments, interests in companies or trusts), you will now appreciate the importance of having access to that information.

In many relationships, one partner handles the major financial transactions while the other manages money for shopping, personal spending and day-to-day costs. In these situations the 'non-finance' partner often knows very little about the property of the parties – who owns what, where the money is coming from, what are the debts and how are they being paid off? This is a pretty common arrangement in many Australian families today.

This situation provides an opportunity for one person to hide, or simply fail to disclose all of the assets when the discussion gets around to the financial settlement after separation. It also leaves one of the parties vulnerable to liabilities or debts that they were entirely unaware of (sometimes known as 'sexually transmitted debt').

The court has taken a consistently tough line on the obligation to make a full and frank disclosure of all assets, liabilities and other financial resources. In fact, if you are asking the court to make any kind of property orders, you must swear that you have made a full disclosure in the documents that you file in the court.

Additionally, the court has wide-ranging and effective powers to enforce disclosure – including the power to compel production of documents (anything that has been 'published' – paper, soft-copy, electronic, disks etc). It can even issue an order that enables the compulsory seizure of documents to ensure they are preserved. Orders can be made against third parties, such as banks, financial institutions, employers, trustees and the like, requiring them to produce relevant financial information.

Virtually any document that is not 'privileged' can be requested and it must be produced for inspection.

WHAT IS LEGAL PRIVILEGE?

'Legal professional privilege' or 'Client legal privilege' are terms that refer to the protection of communications (both written and spoken) between you and your lawyer.

It includes confidential communications between you and your lawyer where you are seeking or being provided with legal advice, as well as communications that relate to potential court proceedings. In short, this covers everything that relates to your case you and your lawyer talk about.

However, be warned – the privilege is not absolute and you can waive it (give it up) without meaning to.

If you act as if you no longer intend to keep the communication confidential, then the court may say that you have given up your right to keep that information private. The most common way that this can happen is if you tell a third party what has been said or just make it public to the world generally (for example, on Facebook). So, be careful who you talk to and what medium you use! You might think that talking to your friends or work colleagues about what your lawyer has told you is just having a chat but a court may see it differently.

Failing to disclose assets

The courts are particularly harsh in dealing with anyone who is found to have failed to make full and frank disclosure of their financial circumstances. Usually there is a significant reduction in what that person might otherwise have received in a property distribution.

If you have not disclosed the details of property owned overseas, the court can take that property into account, make its own assumptions about the value of the property (be it real estate, valuables, investments, bank accounts or any other form of property) and deduct that amount, or whatever it considers appropriate, from your final distribution.

Possible impact on court orders or Financial Agreements

The court has the power to overturn orders or a Financial Agreement and make new orders if you have not made a full and frank disclosure.

For example, if you fail to disclose an interest in a property in the name of a company you have a controlling interest in (such as through a trust controlled by a friend or relative) and the non-disclosure came to the notice of your former partner after orders had been made, he or she could apply to have those orders overturned.

There is no time limit for the court to exercise this power. In other words, if your non-disclosure is found out decades after you thought you had finalised everything, the court may still change the original orders.

A FEW CASES OF WARNING

Disclosure of your financial assets, in EVERY detail, is one of the most important things you have to do in financial matters in the Family Courts.

In a case known as Weir, the husband had been pocketing cash profits from the family business towards the end of the marriage. As a result, the value of the business was significantly reduced. The husband did not tell the court about the extra money and, when questioned about the value of the business, he lied.

Initially, the assets were split 50/50 but when the wife appealed the decision with information about the husband's deceitful conduct, the court decided that she should get an adjustment in her favour – i.e. some of the money back. She received an extra $50,000 plus half of her legal costs.

In the case of Suiker, the husband and wife had come to an agreement on how to divide their property. After the agreement (but before it was lodged in court), the husband was told by his employer that his superannuation would increase from

$27,000 to $162,000 if he accepted redundancy. He failed to tell the wife and the consent orders were made by the court. Six months later, the husband was duly made redundant and received $162,000. When the wife found out, she went back to the court and asked for new orders. The judge awarded the wife an extra $45,000.

The moral is – tell the truth and the whole truth about your financial circumstances.

The consequences of non-disclosure may be dire and, given the enormous power of the Family Courts to examine your financial affairs, the chances of being caught are high. Don't take the risk. Disclose all of your financial information and get matters resolved and settled properly.

Some specific issues to consider regarding property settlement

The laws around property issues are extensive. When deciding how to deal with your finances after separation, you may want to consider the following:

Legal costs in family matters

The standard rule in family law matters is that each person, or party, pays their own legal costs.

However, in certain circumstances, the court may order one party to pay the other party's legal costs. These are known as party-party costs.

In the Federal Magistrates Court, the rules about party-party costs are set out in the Federal Magistrates Court Rules 2001. If you are in the Family Court, these rules are found in Family Law Rules 2004.

The amount of party-party costs that must be paid is determined either by a fixed schedule of costs set by each court (also known as 'the scale'), or by another method chosen by the court. Generally, the court takes into account the following:

▸ the financial circumstances of each party

▸ the conduct of the parties in the proceedings

▸ whether either party has failed to comply with previous court orders

- whether any settlement offer has been made

- any false allegation or statement in the proceedings, and

- any other fact relevant to the case.

If the conduct of one person is particularly obstructive, or is such that it warrants a harsher penalty, the court may order you to pay all of the other person's costs 'reasonably and properly incurred'. These are known as indemnity costs.

The treatment of legal expenses can be quite complex and you should always obtain legal advice about how money spent on your lawyer will be treated in the property distribution.

Disposing of property and the concept of 'add-back'

A court may 'add-back' to the asset pool any amount spent by a party that should have formed part of the property pool.

You should not sell or dispose of any asset before a property settlement has taken place without agreement from the other party or from the court, even though the asset may be in your name alone. Remember, until the property has been legally distributed between you, "what is mine is ours, what is yours is ours and what is ours is ours"!

If you do dispose of property without prior approval, the value of that property may be 'added back' to your share of the proceeds on distribution. In other words, you will be regarded as having already received the value of that property as part of your final entitlement. Take, for example, a situation where you are entitled to a 50/50 share and the total assets are worth $200,000. If you remove $50,000 from a bank account and fail to account for it, your property distribution will probably be reduced to $50,000 (50 per cent equals $100,000, less the $50,000 you are 'deemed' to have received).

This situation can arise if one party deals with property for their own benefit – that is, removes or disposes of property that would otherwise be part of the assets available for division between both of you. The general rule is that assets that were dealt with unfairly or spent for one person's benefit should be considered as already received in the property settlement by the party who received the benefit (and added back). This may apply whether the assets were dealt with in such a way before or after separation.

A court will not automatically add back an amount just because it has been spent. Each case will be considered on its own facts and the court will always look at the circumstances of how the money was spent. One party may have savings at separation but no income to pay day-to-day living expenses. It is most unlikely that a court would consider the spending of this money as an improper reduction of the assets to be added back as part of your share. The court is unlikely to add back where the assets are used to meet reasonable daily needs.

As a general rule, if you lose (or gain) money or assets during the relationship, the losses (or gains) will be shared between you. Under some circumstances, one of you may be held responsible for losses (but it will be rare for one party only to benefit from the wins). You may be held responsible, for example, if one of you acted deliberately to reduce the value of an asset, or acted 'recklessly, negligently or wantonly', resulting in a reduction in value.

The same may apply to any assets disposed of between separation and final settlement. If you dispose of an asset for your own benefit, the value of that asset might be added back to the asset pool.

There are many different situations where the court has decided to 'add back' the value of assets; for example, giving an asset to a friend for no charge, gambling joint money away or losses from failed business ventures.

Even using joint money to buy property that may decline in value, such as vehicles, boats or electronic goods, may be added back.

After separation, you may use joint money to pay legal costs. Legal fees are considered a reasonable expense and they generally will not be added back into the asset pool. However, each case is decided on its own facts and there may be an adjustment where one party spends significantly more than the other on their lawyers.

DRINK YOUR WINE, DON'T COLLECT IT

In one case, after separation, the husband used joint funds to buy a $1.8 million wine collection. At the time of trial, the wine was valued at $1.2 million.

The husband explained that he was aware of the short-term losses involved with the investment, but felt they were outweighed by the long-term gain.

The wife argued that despite the long-term investment, the purchase of the wine unfairly removed $600,000 from the asset pool and should therefore be 'added back'.

The court agreed with the wife and determined that his conduct had denied the wife her proper share of the assets. $600,000 was added back and treated as property already distributed to the husband.

Deliberately reducing the value of property

Separation usually places people under stress and they often behave accordingly. Be aware that behaviour that has the effect of reducing the value (or existence) of the assets may have serious consequences. It may attract the 'add back' principle.

The Family Court will take into account the conduct of a person who deliberately reduces the value of or wastes, property. Selling the husband's boat or the new Honda for $1 is not recommended, nor is slashing the leather furniture with a razor or throwing your hard-earned cash across the tables at the casino. In a celebrated case, an aggrieved wife threw all her husband's antique furniture and tapestries into the swimming pool and then topped it up with several cans of black paint. The Family Court thought this was 'waste' and deducted the value of those assets (and the costs of cleaning up the pool) from her final property settlement.

DON'T THROW IT AWAY

In a case known as Kowaliw, the Family Court concluded that financial losses in the course of a marriage should be shared by the parties (although not necessarily equally) except:

▶ *where one of them behaved in a way that was designed to reduce or minimise the value of assets, or*

▶ *where one of them had acted recklessly, negligently or wantonly in a way that had reduced the value of assets.*

In other words, if you throw it away, by your own conduct, you will be responsible for any losses and the value of the loss will be deducted from your final entitlement.

Where one person deliberately incurs business losses, the value of those losses may be added back to the asset pool.

Gambling losses can be a little more complicated and, again, each case will depend on its own facts. It can be difficult to maintain an argument that gambling losses should be added back, especially if both enjoyed gambling as a form of entertainment, or if gambling was generally accepted by the couple as a form of entertainment during the relationship, even if it was only done by one of them.

Setting aside transactions

Just because you have transferred or got rid of some assets does not necessarily mean you have put them beyond the reach of the other partner or the jurisdiction of the Family Courts.

The courts have very wide powers over financial transactions. This includes the power to **reverse transactions** that have already been made where those transactions may have an impact on the property distribution between the parties.

For example, the sale of a property to a relative might be cancelled by the court and the original owner reinstated, even though the transfer may have been registered and money changed hands. Transfers out of a bank account might be reversed and an order made for the bank to reinstate the money back to the original account.

This also applies to the sale of shares, the appointment of a director in a company and the distribution of profits from a trust. There is no limit to what transactions might be affected, so long as they have had an impact on the possible distribution of the assets between ex-partners.

Capital Gains Tax (CGT) can be a trap

Capital Gains Tax is not payable on the transfer of property if the transfer is done by a property distribution under the *Family Law Act*.

However, be careful. You may end up with an investment property or some other asset that has increased in value since it was bought. When the property is sold, you will be responsible for payment of all the CGT (which was deferred at the time it was transferred to you as part of the property distribution).

These tax implications should be taken into account when negotiating a property distribution that involves assets where CGT may apply – and that's not just real estate.

If neither party is willing to assume the CGT risk, you should seek to have the relevant asset sold and CGT taken into account as a liability of both parties. The family home will not usually have CGT implications and it may be advantageous to seek to retain this asset.

Tax liabilities are a potential minefield and need to be carefully thought out. Therefore, you should get sound advice on these issues from your accountant.

Superannuation and pension entitlements

In 2002, the government decided that superannuation would become part of family law. The *Family Law Act* was changed and the law began to treat superannuation as 'property' and consider it as part of the property distribution process for separated married parties. In 2009, this was extended to separated de facto couples.

Since then, either partner's superannuation and/or pension entitlements can be divided up ('split') and transferred to the other partner as part of a financial distribution.

Pensions are treated as an asset in much the same way as superannuation, even pensions you were entitled to before or during the relationship, or since it has ended. And this includes not just lump-sum pension entitlements but pensions paid as income in periodic instalments.

A superannuation interest (or a pension) is valued using formulas set out in the relevant laws and regulations.

Under family law, you are entitled to receive details of the current value of your former partner's entitlements.

Superannuation division, or 'super splitting' can only be achieved:

▶   by way of a court order (for example, as part of an Application for Consent Orders) or

▶   by private agreement through a Superannuation Agreement (which forms part of a Financial Agreement – see chapter 7 'Contracting out of the family law system – Financial Agreements').

You can also 'quarantine' or protect superannuation for a defined time (called a 'flagging order'). 'Flagging' has the effect of freezing the distribution or payment of superannuation entitlements until a split has been done.

There may be times when it is not a good idea to split a superannuation entitlement and where you may want to protect your interest for a future split. You can 'flag' your interest by a court order, which would then be provided to the trustee of the fund. The trustee would then be legally prohibited from distributing any funds under that policy until the court lifts the order (or it is discharged by the appropriate split).

How is superannuation adjusted?

When a party has superannuation entitlements, the court (or the parties) can make an order to split or quarantine any amount of the super for the other party. Alternatively, non-superannuation assets may be adjusted to compensate one party for the fact that the other party has greater superannuation entitlements.

The options are:

1. Making a splitting order

Superannuation is split from (taken out of) one fund and transferred to another fund nominated by the other partner – either an existing fund or a new one created for that distribution. When superannuation is split from a fund, the person who used to have the super loses all interest and entitlement in the amount that is split off.

2. Making a flagging order

An order is made preventing the trustee of the superannuation fund from dealing with a specified entitlement until some event (usually retirement, when a party becomes entitled to access their superannuation). At that date, the trustee will have to comply with whatever is in the order – usually a payment made to the other person based on a percentage of the value of the superannuation when that event occurs. This option may be appropriate where someone is close to retirement or there are difficulties valuing the superannuation before the relevant date, or where the superannuation is expected to increase at a faster rate as retirement nears.

3. Adjusting non-superannuation property as a compensation

The other assets are adjusted to take into account the difference in superannuation entitlements. For example, instead of dividing up the superannuation, one party may be given a greater percentage distribution in the financial settlement than they would have been entitled to (under the 1, 2 and 3 principle).

You can negotiate with your ex-partner with any of these approaches. The approach that suits you may depend on the difference between your superannuation entitlements and your ex's – the greater the difference, the more challenging the negotiation may be. Often, especially in longer relationships, parties will agree to 'equalise' their superannuation entitlements by splitting off an amount from the party with the greater amount of super to bring the other party up to the same level. For example, if John has super worth $200,000 and Jane's is worth $100,000, John splits $50,000 out of his super to Jane and they both end up with $150,000 in super entitlements.

Types of superannuation interests

There are three main types of superannuation interest (or entitlement):

> ▸ An **accumulation entitlement** is a super interest where you put money into a fund controlled by an independent trustee. Your contributions (and any by your employer) are invested for capital and income growth. You receive a payout (as a lump sum or as a periodic pension) when you retire. With this type of superannuation, it is fairly easy to find out the value by reference to your most recent superannuation statement.

> ▸ A **defined benefit interest** is where your entitlements are controlled by an independent trustee and the value is determined on your retirement. That value will be based on such things as the number of years of employment, your level of seniority and salary at retirement and contributions you may have made. It is often difficult to know the value of these super entitlements until they 'vest' (mature or are paid out) but there are methods of valuation required for family law purposes.

> ▸ A **self-managed superannuation** fund is quite different from the above types of funds as the trustees are normally the persons who are entitled to receive the superannuation when it becomes available. The value of the fund will be determined by valuing the fund's assets at the date of distribution of property under family law. It is important that accurate details of these assets are obtained to enable the distribution to be fair and reasonable.

The valuation of accumulation and defined benefit funds can usually be obtained directly from your fund by sending what is a 'Form 6 Superannuation Information Request'. These forms are available on most superannuation trustee websites and the Family Court website. Most funds charge a processing fee, usually between $50 and $100. The funds must comply with a request for information.

Get legal and financial advice about superannuation

Unless you have a working knowledge of superannuation and this area of family law, you really should get advice before attempting to divide superannuation. It is complex and requires professional financial advice. It also demands specialised legal expertise to draft orders or an agreement, as complicated and specific procedures must be followed.

When splitting superannuation, you might be dealing with quite substantial amounts. It would be worth the expense of engaging your accountant or financial adviser and a specialist family lawyer to get it right.

A last word about finalising property distribution by agreement

With financial matters – whether you are married or in a de facto relationship – you have the freedom to make an arrangement between yourselves without going to court. You don't have to use lawyers.

You can either add up all of your assets and the liabilities and divide the balance between yourselves, in whatever proportion is agreed – or it can be decided by a court. The court deals with these issues every day and knows how to handle them, even if you can't.

Settle sooner, rather than later

You can start negotiating a property settlement from the moment you separate. Consider the following:

▶ The sooner you start, the more likely you are to reach an agreement with your former partner.

▶ Discussions between the two of you are a lot cheaper than an argument conducted by lawyers.

▶ The more you spend on lawyers, the less you will have to divide between yourselves.

▶ It is better to compromise early – sometimes even settling for less than you thought was the worst possible scenario – rather than see even more of your assets frittered away in legal fees and court costs.

Legal fees

It is very important to realise that there are usually no winners in the Family Courts and paying your own legal expenses is the normal outcome.

So, you must consider the costs you will incur in running a legal case. Remember, also, that legal fees for family law matters are not tax deductible.

Legal fees are discussed in more detail in chapter 10 'The elephant in the room – legal costs in family law matters'.

Use lawyers to draft financial agreements and consent orders

Get lawyers involved to draw up any agreements you're able to reach as Financial Agreements or consent orders and get advice about how to ensure the documents are legal and enforceable.

If you shop around, you should be able to get a fixed fee quote for this work. Although the cost may be several thousand dollars, this is not out of proportion to the work required or the outcome that you will achieve – especially compared with the enormous expense of preparing for and going through a court case.

Litigation might cost you tens (if not hundreds) of thousands of dollars and, even at the end of the case, you might not get anywhere near what you wanted because the court did not see things your way.

An agreement reached between you will:

- ▸ slash your legal bills to a fraction of the cost of court actions
- ▸ reduce the time your life is placed on hold, and
- ▸ immediately ease the stress and tensions on you and your family (without such an agreement, you may have to wait several years for a final outcome).

Whatever happens, do not let your lawyer commence court action without telling you about the costs and the likely results. If you can identify the issues early on, you can probably discuss them and negotiate a reasonable settlement, which you can then document as consent orders or as a Financial Agreement.

On the other hand, if you have millions of dollars worth of assets and you and your ex-partner are in dispute over 10 per cent of the value of those assets, you may think it is worthwhile to battle it out in court.

In some cases, particularly where the issues are extremely complex (if, for example, the value of complicated involvement in business ventures is in question), the courts may have to get involved to sort them out.

TIPS ABOUT PROPERTY ISSUES

▶ *Keep as much of the personal property as you can. The cost of replacing personal property will always vastly exceed its 'value' in family law calculations (which is second-hand auction value – a brand new fridge that cost you $1,500 might be worth $500 if you auction it).*

▶ *It is often advantageous to get matters settled as soon as possible after a separation – especially if the other person is feeling responsible for what happened. Conversely, be careful of making a settlement when you feel guilty or responsible for the breakdown of a relationship.*

▶ *There are lots of ways of splitting personal property (furniture, paintings, cookware etc). My favourite is the 'Mexican standoff' where one party submits two lists of the property and the other selects which list comprises the property they want to keep. Another method is 'coloured spots', where each party has a box of coloured sticky spots and you take turns to put a spot on an item of property until every item has your or their colour on it (which you then get to keep in the settlement).*

▶ *Get financial advice about how realistic proposals are. You may really want to keep the family home, but if you don't have the income to pay off the mortgage, it may not be practical for you to do so. Even if you can pay off the house with your income after the split, how much will be left over for you to live on?*

▶ *You may want to stay in the home but can't afford it now. See if you can agree that the property will be sold at some time in the future with you receiving a lower percentage of that sale than you might be entitled to if it took place straight away. For example, you might agree with your ex that you will keep the house until the youngest child turns 18 and then sell it, but instead of getting 40 per cent of the profit now, you might get 30 per cent in five years, to offset your use of the property over those five years.*

▶ *Make sure you get legal advice quickly if there is a danger that your ex-partner might dispose of an asset you might not be able to get back. Although some things can be 'added back' into the pool (as discussed earlier on page 80), specific items might be personally irreplaceable to you.*

▶ *Don't think you can remove property from a distribution by transferring it out of your name or 'giving' it to another person. The court has the power to slice right through these sorts of manoeuvres and, even if the property is not added back the transaction might simply be reversed.*

IT'S ONLY FAIR – CHILD SUPPORT

SUMMARY

- Parents have a responsibility to contribute to the costs of looking after their children.

- The Child Support Agency (CSA) is responsible for determining the amount and distribution of child support from one parent to another.

- The system and formulas for child support are complicated and based not only on what each of you earns but on how much time is spent with the children.

- You can make a private agreement to replace the CSA amount, or to have it paid by providing specific support such as school fees or medical expenses, rather than cash.

Once you and your ex have split, you probably need to come to some reasonably quick decisions about arrangements for funding your children's expenses (schooling, medical, day-to-day living expenses and so on).

Child support is the payment of money by one parent to another parent or carer, or for the benefit of a child.

- The child support system is complex and the best advice we can give you is to contact the Child Support Agency (directly or through its excellent website) to get the specific information you require to understand your entitlements or liabilities. The following chapter provides some pointers about how the system works and how it might affect you.

- Either parent can apply for a child support assessment. However, it is worth doing the calculations first. You may expect to receive money, yet end up actually owing money.

▸ An estimator of child support payments is available on the CSA website (www.csa.gov.au). Input details of your income, your partner's income and how much time each spends with the children and it will estimate how much you will owe or receive.

▸ Child support is then assessed by the CSA by applying a formula set down by law.

▸ The key elements of the formula are:

- the costs of raising children

- the incomes of both parents (these are taken into account and considered equally), and

- the amount of care each parent provides (the time a child spends with each parent).

▸ An allowance is then made for the needs of each party for their own support.

▸ The CSA then issues its administrative assessment setting out who pays how much to the other and a calculation is made showing the balance owing by one parent. This is the child support amount.

▸ In many cases the CSA collects the money and distributes it, so that the former couple does not have to manage or control it themselves. However, it is possible to have a private payment arrangement where the money is transferred directly rather than through the Child Support Agency.

You can make a private agreement (a Child Support Agreement) in certain circumstances. This replaces the 'administrative assessment'.

Background to the child support system

The child support system was set up in 1989 and is covered by the *Child Support Assessment Act* and the *Child Support Registration & Collection Act*. The scheme is administered by the Child Support Agency (CSA).

The Child Support Agency is responsible for "... supporting separated parents to transfer payments for the benefit of their children."

The child support system is designed to keep people out of the courts as much as possible. Although large and bureaucratic, the agency is highly effective at assessing parents' liability to pay child support and administering the system to ensure that the support is paid. Since it was established, the agency has transferred billions of dollars to parents who are looking after their children – making sure that they receive a fair contribution from the other parent.

The CSA has extremely wide powers to access records and tax returns, transfer funds, make assessments and make sure that the money that should be paid is paid. It also has wide powers to enforce collection, such as requiring an employer to deduct child support sums from the wages of a parent for payment to the other parent or intercepting tax refunds.

To determine the actual child support amounts to be paid, the agency applies a formula that takes into consideration financial circumstances and the time children spend with each parent. The formula is quite detailed and seeks to address concerns about the financial impact of the time children spend with each of their parents.

Any parent can seek an assessment from the Child Support Agency and, if an assessment is made, it is legally enforceable. Orders can be obtained to deduct child support payments from salaries. Additionally, payments may be deducted and paid to the agency from tax refunds and Departure Prohibition Orders (DPO) may be issued preventing non-payers from leaving the country.

THE CHILD SUPPORT AGENCY WEBSITE

We recommend you look at the Child Support Agency's website for detailed information about the child support system, potential liabilities and entitlements and to download a range of forms.

www.csa.gov.au

The website also features a helpful guide for people who do not understand the detail and functioning of the system (which is just about everybody).

How child support assessment works

The current child support formula was introduced in 2008. Child support is now based on the actual costs of children and the capacity of both parents to pay those costs (taking into account their respective incomes).

A parent or carer may apply for an administrative assessment of child support, which must then be paid by the parent for a child. The liable (paying) parent includes an adoptive parent or the parent of a child born by artificial conception. It does not include a step parent.

Applications can be made to the Child Support Agency in writing, by phone or online.

When an application is accepted by the agency, it advises each party of the assessment (setting out the amount and the calculations).

A child for whom support may be paid includes:

▶ an adopted child

▶ a child of a separated married couple, and

▶ a child born to an unmarried couple who lived together between 20 and 44 weeks prior to the birth.

Child support ends when a child turns 18. It may also end if the child becomes 'a member of a couple' or is adopted. Child support can be extended to the end of a school year where the child turns 18 in the final year of school.

Some issues concerning child support

The following information may be relevant if you are considering child support.

Paternity – fatherhood of children

If you are the parent of a child, you are liable for the child's support. This is the case whether the child is planned or the result of a one-night stand.

There may be a question about the identity of a child's father and this will have to be resolved before a child support assessment can be made. 'Paternity' is the term used for the fatherhood of a child.

If you are unsure who is the father of your child, or whether you are the father of a child, there are steps you can take through the court to ensure you find out the truth.

The *Family Law Act* presumes a person is the father of a child in certain circumstances including:

▶ where people are married

▶ the parties cohabitated around the presumed date of conception

▶ a person was registered as the father at the time of the birth

▶ there is an acknowledgment of parentage by the father in a written document, or

▶ a court has made a determination that a person is the parent of the child.

The CSA may accept a claim that the other party is a parent if it is satisfied that any of these presumptions have been met.

It is possible to challenge any of these presumptions (but not a determination of parentage by a court).

Where doubt remains, an application may be made to the court to order medical testing to clarify the biological parentage of a child. There must be sufficient evidence to throw doubt on the paternity of a child for the court to order medical testing (usually DNA sampling), and an applicant must have an honest, bona fide and reasonable belief as to the parentage. Usually, the DNA testing will prove conclusively whether someone is the father of a child (99.99 per cent accuracy can be achieved through modern testing methods).

If a person refuses to undergo DNA testing, the courts may conclude that this is evidence of paternity.

DNA testing is not a painful or invasive procedure. It can be done through mouth swabs or a hair sample and it usually takes no more than five to seven working days to determine. It costs around $300. It is also possible to test for DNA using items such as cigarette butts, cutlery or sperm samples.

When the court has considered the evidence provided, it will make a declaration of parentage. Such a declaration is proof in Australia that the named person is the father of the child in question (and, as a result, will be potentially liable to pay child support).

Salary sacrifices and investment losses

If you salary sacrifice superannuation contributions, these will be included as part of your child support income to work out how much you should pay (or receive). So, too, will net investment losses.

The exclusion of extra income after separation

Additional income you make after separation may be excluded from the child support assessment – for example, if you have a second job or worked overtime.

Care arrangements

Where a paying parent has regular care of a child, their liability will be reduced because of the direct contribution made by that parent to the cost of raising the child. There are two possibilities:

> ▸ **Regular care**. If your children live with you between two and five nights a fortnight, and you are the paying parent, your payments will be reduced because you are directly contributing to the cost of raising a child through that care time.

> ▸ **Shared care**. If each parent has between five and nine nights a fortnight, child support is adjusted even further and both parents may receive family assistance payments to help them with the cost of children.

However, if you only have daytime contact and do not spend any nights with your child, this time will not count for the purposes of the assessment.

Income estimates

If you are the paying parent and your income falls by 15 per cent or more, you can lodge an estimate of income. If the child support registrar accepts your estimate, your child support will be adjusted according to the new taxable income amount. Beware if your estimate is incorrect, because there may be a significant re-adjustment at the end of the relevant tax year.

If you are unhappy with an assessment

Under limited circumstances, you can take an objection regarding child support to the courts. First, you must lodge an objection with the child support registrar for a change in the assessment. This objection must be lodged within 28 days of the assessment, although there is provision for objections out of time.

If the child support registrar rejects your objection, you may apply to the Social Security Appeals Tribunal (SSAT) for a review. If you remain dissatisfied with the outcome, you can make a further appeal to the Administrative Appeals Tribunal.

However, this is not the appropriate route for objections on the basis of parentage. If your objection is based on your belief that the agency has not assessed the true parents of the child, an application should be lodged with the court either for a determination on the basis of the *Family Law Act* presumptions of paternity (as set out earlier in this chapter under the heading 'Some issues concerning child support') or to order DNA testing.

Keeping the CSA informed

The easiest way you can ensure your assessment is correct is to keep the Child Support Agency advised of any change in circumstances including:

▶ care arrangements for the children

▶ the number of dependent children for whom you might be responsible

▶ any change in your income, or

▶ the occurrence of any event that may terminate the current arrangements.

KEEPING UP WITH CHANGES IN CHILD SUPPORT

The child support sssessment scheme provides for independent assessment of both parties' incomes to establish which parent, if either, should be paying child support to the other parent.

This is done through a complex formula, which considers a number of factors including how many nights per week the child spends with each parent and the overall income of each parent.

More information can be found on the Child Support Agency website:
www.csa.gov.au

On the website, you can apply for child support and obtain an estimate of what payments would be assessed if you did apply for child support.

Child maintenance after a child turns 18

There are some situations where financial support for a child may be payable after they turn 18. For example, where the caring parent is unable to adequately support a child where the 'child' is over 18 and has a disability or is in tertiary education. Such support is not assessed by the Child Support Agency but is ordered under the *Family Law Act*.

If you find yourself supporting such a 'child', you should consult a lawyer to get information and advice about your entitlements or responsibilities.

Payment and collection of child support

The CSA can collect the child support payments or you can arrange payment directly between yourselves.

If you choose, you can collect and transfer child support payments, by agreement, directly out of the paying partner's wages and into the receiving partner's bank account.

Child Support Agreements

If both parents agree, you can enter into a private child support arrangement by way of Child Support Agreement. Provided the agreement complies with all of the relevant requirements, the CSA will usually accept it.

Child Support Agreements must be formally registered with the CSA. They are binding on each of the parents and prevent the agency from making an assessment.

According to the Child Support Agency:

> " ... a child support agreement offers parents a flexible way of arranging child support. If you can both agree on how your children should be supported financially, you can make a child support agreement and ask us to accept it. You can ask us to collect and transfer child support payments, or you can do it without our help.
>
> "There are some conditions that must be met before we can accept a child support agreement. For example, parents who agree to less child support than the amount assessed under the child support formula can do so as long as they get legal advice."

There are two types of agreements, limited agreements and binding agreements, which vary in a number of ways.

Limited Child Support Agreement

- ▶ can be terminated after three years if either party wishes, or at any time if financial circumstances have significantly changed

- ▶ require a child support assessment to already be in place

- ▶ the amount payable under the new agreement cannot be less than under the CSA assessment

- ▶ must be in writing, signed by both parents and lodged with the CSA, and

- ▶ you do not need independent legal advice before signing.

A Limited Child Support Agreement may be terminated

> ▶ after three years, by written application to the CSA

> ▶ if the CSA's notional assessment of how much child support would be paid without the agreement changes by 15 per cent (either positively or negatively), or

> ▶ by applying to the court to set the agreement aside.

Binding Child Support Agreement

> ▶ Each parent must obtain independent legal advice about the advantages and disadvantages of the agreement and what effect it will have on their rights, before they sign.

> ▶ Each parent's lawyer must provide a statement that they provided the independent legal advice.

> ▶ After the agreement is signed, a copy of the agreement must be given to each parent.

> ▶ The agreement can be made for any amount that the parents agree to, including amounts less than the formula assessment.

> ▶ There does not have to be a child support formula assessment already in place.

A Binding Child Support Agreement can only be ended before the children turn 18 (when it concludes in any event) by:

> ▶ a termination agreement

> ▶ a new binding agreement, or

> ▶ a court order setting it aside.

A court order setting aside the agreement (which will require an application to the Federal Magistrates Court or the Family Court) is not easy to obtain and will not be made simply on the basis that you have changed your mind.

Which type of agreement is best?

A Limited Child Support Agreement is likely to be the best option for you, if you think that your circumstances may change in the future (either financially or in terms of time spent with the children), or there is a long period of time before the children turn 18.

It is far easier to renegotiate or opt out of a Limited Agreement if, and when, circumstances change, than it is with a Binding Agreement.

This is also the best option if you are not confident that your income, or your ex-partner's income, will remain pretty much the same in the future – either up or down. Limited Agreements can be ended by one person if the CSA assessment changes more than 15 per cent in either direction (as a result of income changes or care arrangements).

On the other hand, if you are concerned that your partner may change their mind down the track and you want the certainty of consistent, regular payments set in concrete, a Binding Child Support Agreement might be a good idea.

This is also an option worth considering if your children are teenagers and there is not long to go before child support will end.

A Binding Child Support Agreement will also be the best option if you and your partner agree that less child support should be paid than the CSA assessment indicates, which may occur if one person is supporting the other and the children in a way that is not taken into account by the CSA calculations. (However, remember that payment of school fees, medical fees etc, are also considered by the CSA.)

A Binding Child Support Agreement might be set aside by the Family Courts in certain circumstances. These include:

▶ where your agreement was obtained by fraud or a failure to disclose information that is relevant

▶ where one of the parties to the agreement (or someone acting for one of the parties):

- exerted undue influence or duress in obtaining that agreement, or

- engaged in unconscionable or other conduct to such an extent that it would be unjust not to set aside the agreement, or

- exceptional circumstances have arisen since the agreement was made and a party or the child will suffer hardship if the agreement is not set aside.

Advantages of a Child Support Agreement

▶ an agreement gives parents the ability to determine child support arrangements without involving the CSA (except for registration)

> ▸ an agreement provides a greater level of certainty for your child support entitlements (and liabilities) into the future

> ▸ you have a consistent level of child support over time, which will help both parties in financial planning, and

> ▸ you have the ability to earn a higher income without reducing or increasing the level of your child support.

Possible disadvantages of a Child Support Agreement

> ▸ agreements are difficult to terminate and you will not be able to unilaterally end the agreement in the future, and

> ▸ there are potential legal costs associated with a termination agreement or court application.

The child support assessment formula – for those who are into puzzles

If you wish to understand the process for calculating child support, try working through the following steps:

The formula

This basic child support assessment formula applies to parents with one child and no other dependent children. The assessment is calculated like this:

1. **Work out your child support income**

   This is your taxable income less the 'parenting self-support amount' indexed annually. The 'parenting self support amount' for 2011 is $20,594.

2. **Work out the combined child support income**

   This is both parents' child support income amounts added together.

3. **Work out your income percentage**

   This is the amount you got from Question 1, as a percentage of the amount you got from Question 2.

4.   **Work out your care percentage**

This is based on the number of nights in a year that the child lives with each parent, expressed as a percentage of the year.

5.   **Work out your cost percentage**

This is calculated from your answer to Question 4. You take the care percentage and check which category it fits into (these are set out on the CSA's website and range from 0 per cent to <14 per cent up to >86 per cent to 100 per cent).

6.   **Work out your child support percentage**

This is each parent's income percentage (see Question 3) minus their cost percentage (Question 5).

If the percentage is positive, you need to pay child support. If the percentage is negative, you are entitled to receive child support.

7.   **Work out the cost of your child**

This is calculated using a table on the CSA website that is updated every year. It takes into account your combined child support income and then takes the cost of each child as a percentage of that number.

8.   **Work out the child support amount**

Multiply the liable parent's child support percentage (Question 6) by the cost of the child (Question 7). This gives the amount the liable parent will have to pay per year.

It should be pretty obvious that child support calculations are not for the mathematically challenged!

It really is much easier to use the calculator on the CSA's website or to contact the agency to get advice.

CHILD SUPPORT TELEPHONE RESOURCES

Child Support Agency

CSA Info Service (Auto Service for Quick Account)	13 12 72
Enquiries and General Information	13 11 07
CSA Complaints	13 29 19
Change of Assessment (Review)	13 14 11

GETTING IT SETTLED
– IT'S IN YOUR INTERESTS

SUMMARY

▶ Negotiating a settlement agreement with your former partner that both of you can live with is likely to save you a lot of money, time and stress.

▶ Settling will be quicker, easier, cheaper and probably get you closer to what you want than a court decision will.

▶ If possible, it is best to stay out of court and sort things out between you.

▶ If you and your former partner are already in agreement, or close to agreement, lawyers can help you get settlements done in a legal way without going to court.

▶ If you think you could reach an agreement but emotions are running high or there are a few things that you can't figure out together, you may wish to consider mediation or hiring a lawyer to help you find new ways to resolve the situation.

▶ Even if you go to court, you can still decide to come to an agreement with your ex. This can be done even in the middle of a trial – though obviously, earlier is better (and thousands of dollars cheaper).

Getting matters settled by negotiated agreement is almost always in everybody's best interests. It may be hard (as emotions are raw after a separation) but, if it can be achieved, the outcome is likely to be much better than the alternatives.

This raises two important questions:

> *Why* should you seek to settle by negotiated agreement?

> *How* can you achieve that agreement?

Why try to settle?

A negotiated agreement has many advantages:

> It gives you finality and certainty. You can then get on with your life knowing what your financial future is likely to be and what arrangements are in place for the kids.

> It minimises the risks of the court process. No lawyer can promise you what result they will achieve at the end of the process – there are too many unknowns.

> Kids will not have to live with the ongoing tensions of a court battle (even if it's not about them).

> Family and close friends will not get dragged into an ongoing battle.

> Resolution will be much quicker. Going through the court system can take years (although many matters are resolved earlier).

> It will definitely be much less expensive. Lawyers normally charge by the amount of time they spend on your matter, not by the results they achieve. So, the longer your matter goes on, the more it will cost.

> Starting litigation means you are handing over decisions on important financial and children's issues to somebody else – namely, the judge. You therefore no longer have any control over the outcome.

> The legal costs saved by early compromise may more than compensate for the amount that you 'gave away'.

> In children's matters, a reasonable compromise may well mean that the arrangements work more smoothly for everyone – even though you may have less time with the children than you originally wanted.

How to settle

The chart below shows how the steps to a final agreed settlement might proceed.

 ▸ After separation you negotiate a settlement.

 ▸ Successful negotiation leads to:

 - an agreement (financial or child support), or

 - consent orders (financial and children's matters).

 ▸ These are then 'registered' in the Family Courts (or exclude the courts from becoming involved), and

 ▸ The matter is finalised.

Steps to settlement

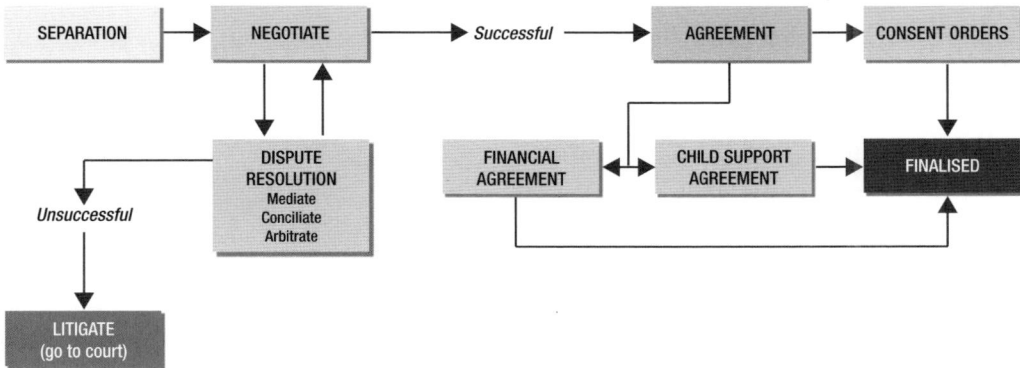

The practicalities of settlement

Negotiated settlement

A negotiated settlement means that you determine the terms of agreement, with or without legal or other professional help (such as mediators). That agreement is then converted into a document that is legally binding.

The agreement is then either registered in court as consent orders and becomes a final and enforceable contract between you, or (where only financial matters are involved) it may be written up as a Financial Agreement and signed by all parties and their lawyers to become final and enforceable. Financial Agreements are discussed in more detail in chapter 7 'Contracting out of the family law system'. If both parents agree, Child Support Agreements (as discussed in chapter 5 'It's only fair – child support') can be determined in much the same way and registered with the CSA.

You can, of course, simply come to an informal agreement with your ex (whether it's in writing or not) and get on with your business. But such an agreement would not be binding or enforceable (see the box below 'A warning about informal agreements' that follows).

A WARNING ABOUT INFORMAL AGREEMENTS

You can reach an agreement with your ex-partner – in writing or not – and leave it at that.

This is an 'informal agreement'. It can be witnessed by the local JP or you can just rely on a verbal understanding about how you will sort things out.

An informal agreement is not binding on the parties and is not legally enforceable.

Whether the agreement will work depends entirely on the continuing good faith of both parties. If one decides they don't like the agreement and decides to take it to court, the informal agreement is nothing more than evidence of your intention at the time it was made.

It is very important to know that either party may seek to have entirely new arrangements made at some later date by applying to the court.

For any agreement to be a legally binding agreement under family law it must be:

- ▸ *'registered' in the court by way of consent orders, or*
- ▸ *executed (signed) as a Financial Agreement in accordance with the law.*

Settlement – how to get it done properly

You can achieve virtually anything by an agreement with your ex-partner – so long as it involves arrangements for your children and/or property and it's legal!

1. **Firstly**, enter into negotiations with your ex-partner. This is often a difficult thing to do as emotions are high soon after separation. Negotiations usually don't get easier as time progresses and, if you want a negotiated settlement, the sooner you start the better. It is important at this stage to focus on outcomes – getting matters resolved – rather than the blame game of whose fault it was that the relationship did not work. Sometimes, you will only be able to conduct these negotiations through independent and objective third parties.

2. **Secondly**, try to work out the terms of the agreement. You will need to deal with all of the issues that are of concern to you, starting with the ones that are less likely to be in dispute. In this way, you can start building the foundations for agreement with some positive 'can-do' issues, rather than tougher issues that could take longer to resolve.

3. **Thirdly**, get the terms of your understanding put into a legal framework (usually by getting consent orders made by the court) so that the agreement is legally effective and can be implemented in the best possible way. This applies equally to kids' matters as it does to financial issues.

Needing help?

Decide whether you want professional assistance for any or all of these steps.

For example, you might ask whether it's worth:

▶ finding a mediator to assist in your early negotiations

▶ involving your accountant or financial adviser in understanding the implications of specific terms in the agreement

▶ talking to a real estate agent about real estate values and selling or keeping a property

▶ seeking assistance from a counsellor or psychologist to help in dealing with difficult emotional issues that may arise after separation, and/or

▶ getting lawyers involved in drafting up an agreement or explaining the legal implications of what you propose to include.

Without professional legal assistance you may find it quite difficult to finalise your dispute by writing up an agreement as consent orders for lodging in court.

Whether you engage mediators, accountants, lawyers or any other professionals at any stage is really a cost-benefit analysis that only you can decide.

As far as legal involvement is concerned, you might want to think about the following questions:

▶ How much will the lawyers cost? (This is a question you should always ask your lawyer at the outset.)

▶ Is this cost fixed and guaranteed or is it an estimate? If so, what is the top end of the range that you might be asked to pay and are there any caps or limits on what you might be charged?

▶ Are there any additional fees (such as court costs or barristers' fees) to be included and how much are they likely to be?

▶ How much is it worth to have the peace of mind of knowing everything has been finally and legally resolved?

▶ Is it worth the legal expense if the asset pool is relatively modest or you are dealing with quite a simple issue?

▶ Do the arrangements proposed for the children require consideration and careful drafting by a lawyer or are they so straightforward that the expense would not be justified?

- ▶ Are there any complicated issues regarding property that a lawyer should look through?

- ▶ Are you getting a property deal that is fair and reasonable in the eyes of the law that has everything that should be included?

- ▶ Is superannuation involved and, if so, should you be seeking a transfer of part of your ex-partner's super entitlements or should you be giving them part of yours? What should the mix of super and non-super assets be?

- ▶ Are consent orders the best way to go or would a Financial Agreement be more appropriate in your circumstances? If a Financial Agreement is appropriate, each of you must have an independent lawyer or the agreement will not be valid (see chapter 7 'Contracting out of the family law system – Financial Agreements').

At the end of the day, whether or not you involve a lawyer is your decision.

Whatever else you do, don't forget our earlier advice: unless your agreement is prepared in accordance with the requirement of family law, **you do not have a binding and enforceable contract**. Ask yourself the question: "Is it worth running that risk?"

What are consent orders?

Consent orders can be made at any time by the court when proceedings are on foot between parties. They are usually made in one of two circumstances:

- ▶ as a result of filing an Application for consent orders without disputed proceedings, or

- ▶ at any stage during disputed proceedings commenced by one of the parties.

Application for Consent Orders

If you and your ex-partner are able to reach an agreement about children and/ or property distribution (with or without legal assistance), you can file (lodge) that agreement through a process known as an Application for Consent Orders. You can do this yourself, as explained in the following pages. Neither party has to attend court and you simply need to file the document with the court registry.

The court will then review the orders that you are seeking and, in relation to financial and property matters, satisfy itself that the terms of the agreement are 'fair and reasonable' and otherwise appropriate. In other words, the orders will have to comply with the requirements of the *Family Law Act*.

If you have complied with the legal requirements to prepare the forms and the court is satisfied with the terms proposed, it will issue final Consent orders. These amount to a legally binding contract between you and your ex-partner that is enforceable in the court if either party fails to comply with the terms.

Consent orders during court proceedings

After you have commenced proceedings in court, it is still possible to settle any (or all) of the disputed issues by asking the court to make consent orders in whatever terms you agree.

At any stage of proceedings in court, you still have this opportunity to get things finished.

If you are seeking to finalise all of the disputed issues, the court will again want to satisfy itself that the terms are fair and reasonable before issuing final orders and concluding the court process.

If you don't settle

Sometimes, you won't have the opportunity or the ability to negotiate a settlement. For example, if:

> ▸ You and the ex do not agree on the outcome, or you are so far apart that only a court can make the final decision (often when one or both is unreasonable and refuses to compromise).

> ▸ One of you wants to relocate to a place where regular contact with the kids for the other might be very difficult – it's an all or nothing outcome.

> ▸ There is an argument over the facts and you have conflicting positions. This argument could be over almost anything – which parent played the major role in looking after the children or maintaining the home, whether money received from the family company was really a loan or a distribution, whether a winning lottery ticket was bought with joint funds or by a party's mother, etc.

▸ Your ex has already started proceedings in the court. Although you must respond, you still have the option of trying to get matters resolved **at any stage** in the court process by making an offer to settle on terms that you believe are reasonable.

▸ Your ex refuses to engage in negotiation or settlement discussions and court proceedings are commenced to compel them to negotiate or risk having a decision made that may not be in their interests.

▸ There is an urgent need to prevent a party from acting in a certain way – perhaps in the way they look after the kids, or fears that assets will be wasted or liabilities incurred that should not be. The courts can provide speedy answers where negotiation is not a realistic alternative.

It is always best to avoid court proceedings. However, if you can't, then get it over with as soon as possible – as long as the terms are fair and reasonable.

There are only two ways to get matters resolved when a relationship breaks down – by negotiated settlement or through the court process (known as 'litigation').

One of those paths is lengthy, costly and out of your control. The other pathway – negotiated settlement – can be speedy, is certainly less costly and you have a much greater influence over the outcome.

The advantages of settling by agreement are illustrated in the 'family law process flow chart' that follows over the page. This flow chart illustrates the possible steps to resolve a family law matter, from separation (relationship breakdown) to final resolution (final orders). The steps from separation to a negotiated settlement are at the top of the flow chart. Compare this with the convoluted and far more expensive route through the court process at the bottom of the flow chart.

Look how much faster, easier and cheaper it is to head straight along the top of the diagram to a negotiated settlement rather than the costly path of court proceedings (otherwise known as litigation).

Family law process flow chart

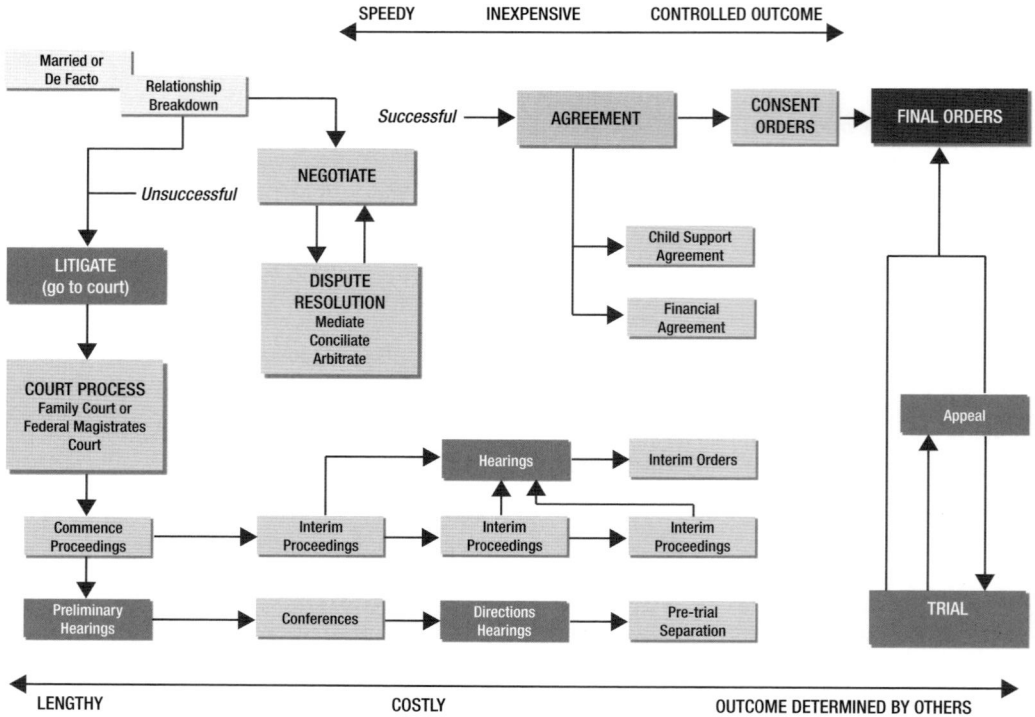

SPEEDY   INEXPENSIVE   CONTROLLED OUTCOME

| Married or De Facto | Relationship Breakdown |
| | Successful → AGREEMENT → CONSENT ORDERS → FINAL ORDERS |

NEGOTIATE

— Unsuccessful

LITIGATE (go to court)

DISPUTE RESOLUTION
Mediate
Conciliate
Arbitrate

Child Support Agreement

Financial Agreement

COURT PROCESS
Family Court or Federal Magistrates Court

Hearings → Interim Orders

Appeal

Commence Proceedings → Interim Proceedings → Interim Proceedings → Interim Proceedings

Preliminary Hearings → Conferences → Directions Hearings → Pre-trial Separation

TRIAL

LENGTHY   COSTLY   OUTCOME DETERMINED BY OTHERS

Litigation – the court process

Litigation is the word used to describe the process of having a matter dealt with in the courts.

It is started by one person approaching the court and asking for decisions about your dispute. Starting the process is usually done by making an application to the court. Your case then proceeds through a number of stages until a decision is made by a judge, which finalises the dispute. The final decision is usually made at or after a trial. It is binding on the parties and is usually referred to as the final orders.

Sometimes, orders will be made along the way to resolve some of the issues in dispute between the parties or how the matter will proceed. Usually called 'interim orders' or 'procedural orders', they are also binding and must be complied with.

If your matter is already in court or has to go there (for whatever reason), chapter 8 'If it positively, definitely has to go to court' gives you some information and advice about how to deal with that.

Settling when the dispute is already in the courts

This chapter is all about resolving your dispute so, we stress again, there is absolutely nothing to prevent you from settling matters at any stage – whether court proceedings have started or not.

If you have lawyers, you can instruct them to put a settlement proposal to the other side. Remember, you are the boss here, not the lawyer. If you reach agreement, you draft up consent orders to finalise some or all of the issues that are before the court. Get the orders 'registered' in court and that part of the dispute is over.

Doing it yourself

If you do decide to go through the settlement process yourself (and whether or not you decide to consult a lawyer or any other professional), there are some possible shortcuts.

Family Court do-it-yourself settlement kits

Go to the court websites and download one of the excellent do-it-yourself kits – which will take you through the steps of preparing and lodging applications and will explain the procedures.

FAMILY COURT DO-IT-YOURSELF SETTLEMENT KITS

The Family Court of Australia kits and further information are available at:
www.familylawcourts.gov.au/wps/wcm/connect/FLC/Home/Forms/Do-it-yourself+kits/

Call 1300 352 000 to speak to someone about using the kits, or visit a Family Court registry.

The Family Court of Western Australia kits are available at:
www.familycourt.wa.gov.au/K/kits.aspx?uid=9932-8552-5939-3858

The Federal Magistrates Court kits are available at:
www.familylawcourts.gov.au/wps/wcm/connect/FLC/Home/Forms/Do-it-yourself+kits/

If using such kits, be careful to follow the steps exactly. Also, be careful that you do not:

▶ mess up your property distribution or your agreement about children in a way that cannot be undone later (without great expense and time)

▶ prepare orders that are impractical or impossible to implement, or

▶ produce orders so complex or confusing that you have to go to court to sort them out anyway.

That is why – unless you are seeking very simple and straightforward orders – it is certainly quicker, safer and probably a lot less expensive in the long term to use a good lawyer to draw up the documents and obtain the consent orders that you need.

At the end of the day, if your lawyer messes it up you may be able to bring an action against him or her for losses you may have suffered. However, if you make a dreadful mistake doing it yourself, you can't really claim compensation.

Other do-it-yourself kits

Several DIY kits (which are not produced by the Family Court) claim to take you through the process of creating and filing consent orders to divide your property or make arrangements for your children. Be careful as they might land you in hot water.

Setting out and documenting proper arrangements for your children and financial distribution can be a minefield for people without professional training and family law knowledge. Many lawyers with years of experience in general practice but no family law specialisation have difficulty giving advice on these matters or negotiating their way through the documentation required.

Doing your own divorce

Do-it-yourself divorce kits are also available on the Family Court website. The site shows you how to access the kits and provides clear explanations and instructions for completing and filing the forms.

The kits contain all of the official forms required to:

- apply for a divorce
- 'serve' your divorce forms, or
- respond to a divorce application.

The divorce kits are pretty easy to use. Most people would be able to obtain a divorce by using them as the process is not terribly complicated. Simply be careful to comply with all of the instructions, fill out the forms exactly as required and follow the procedures carefully.

FILING AND SERVING DIVORCE DOCUMENTS

The Family Law Court website provides a step-by-step guide for filing an Application for Divorce over the internet and serving (delivery) of the documents on your ex-spouse by post or by hand.

Beware, you cannot serve documents personally on an ex-partner.

You can even pay the filing fees online with your credit card.

www.familylawcourts.gov.au/wps/wcm/connect/FLC

When in doubt, get some legal advice. It is likely to be helpful, save you a lot of time and be well worth the dollars you pay for it.

CONTRACTING OUT OF THE FAMILY LAW SYSTEM – FINANCIAL AGREEMENTS

SUMMARY

▶ Financial Agreements can be made before, during or after a marriage or a relationship.

▶ A Financial Agreement sets out how the property will be divided and that's the end of that.

▶ Financial Agreements prevent the courts from intervening in a property distribution (except to overturn the agreement if it is not done properly or deal with property that has not been included in the agreement).

▶ The effect of a valid Financial Agreement will be to stop either party going to the court at a later time to have property divided according to the *Family Law Act*.

▶ These agreements are powerful, complicated documents and they can be expensive to draft and finalise.

▶ There are strict legal requirements that must be complied with for a Financial Agreement to be binding and enforceable in the Family Courts.

▶ You must get advice from a lawyer for a Financial Agreement to be binding and enforceable.

Financial Agreements – what they are and what they do

Financial Agreements are potentially very powerful instruments for determining exactly how financial matters will be resolved if a relationship breaks down.

For all practical purposes, these agreements are the same for marriages and de facto relationships, so we refer to both in this book as Financial Agreements.

Couples (whether in a married or de facto relationship) may make a Financial Agreement to deal with financial arrangements in the event of separation. You can also make arrangements for ongoing financial maintenance for one or both of you in a Financial Agreement.

So, as long as you comply with the provisions of the *Family Law Act,* you can work out yourself how you want to divide things up, rather than worry how the courts might do it.

It is important to know that Financial Agreements prevent the courts from interfering in the arrangements you have made for property division and financial maintenance if you separate. So you are giving up a right that would be available to you in the absence of the agreement.

Sometimes these agreements are referred to as 'pre-nups', but that fails to recognise the much broader circumstances in which they can be made. They are not limited to arrangements you might make before you get married.

These agreements can be made:

> ▶ **before** you enter into a relationship (or marriage)

> ▶ **during** the relationship, or

> ▶ **after** the relationship has ended.

A Financial Agreement need not be 'fair and reasonable' (indeed, it might be very unfair and totally unreasonable) and does not have to divide up your property according to the normal principles of family law (the principles set out in chapter 4 'Dividing up the property – it's as simple as 1, 2, 3'). You can make whatever arrangements you want, provided the Financial Agreement complies with the strict formal requirements set out in the *Family Law Act.*

The requirements for a Financial Agreement include:

▶ Disclosure of the assets and liabilities that are to be covered by the Financial Agreement and all relevant financial information.

▶ Before signing, both parties must have obtained independent legal advice about:

- the effect of the agreement on their rights, and

- the advantages and disadvantages of the agreement.

▶ The agreement must be freely entered into by both parties.

▶ The agreement must be signed by both parties, and

▶ You must have a certificate showing that you have received legal advice about the Financial Agreement. If you do not have this certificate, the Financial Agreement will not be valid.

Financial Agreements can be complex documents and the law places a significant responsibility on lawyers who provide advice about them. As a result, many family lawyers will not touch them.

It can also be expensive to have a lawyer prepare or advise on a Financial Agreement. The cost might be upwards of $2,500 (and in some circumstances much more). Each agreement must specifically reflect a couple's unique circumstances and a heavy onus is placed on the lawyer to comply with the strict requirements of the *Family Law Act*. However, the value and the protection of an agreement may be very significant. It gives you certainty about how things will be dealt with in the event you separate.

Remember, Financial Agreements can only provide for property division and financial maintenance after separation. They cannot deal with issues regarding children or child support.

It is also important to know that if some circumstances change after making the agreement, for example if you have children, it might not be binding. Get advice about these issues.

Why you might want a Financial Agreement

There are many circumstances where a Financial Agreement might be desirable. Some of the more obvious ones include:

▶ to provide certainty regarding the outcome if separation occurs

▶ to avoid arguments down the track

▶ to preserve the ownership of existing property, but share all jointly acquired assets

▶ to preserve an existing or anticipated inheritance

▶ where one party has much greater wealth than the other

▶ in second relationships or marriages where the interests of children from former relationships are to be protected

▶ for asset protection or preservation when there is an early distribution from a potential estate (sometimes called 'inter-generational wealth transfer'), and

▶ trading off a future property distribution against a spousal maintenance arrangement. (For example, one person gets certain property while the other gets the financial security of ongoing financial support).

Inter-generational asset transfers

Sometimes parents want to transfer some of their assets to children as a form of 'early inheritance'. If a transfer is made to a partner in a relationship, the other partner may become entitled to a share of these assets in the event of a separation down the track. Understandably, parents may be reluctant to do the transfer in these circumstances as their intention is to benefit their own child.

The parents can gain some protection if the assets they intend to transfer are included in a Financial Agreement between the couple in a relationship.

Why you might not want to enter into Financial Agreement

One of the potential difficulties with Financial Agreements is that they require a prediction about your financial position at some unknown time in the future if you separate. This is clearly an almost impossible task. Any number of events could intervene to influence the actual position – for example, serious injury to you or your partner, loss of income, unexpected windfalls or changes in family circumstances.

If you separate **without** an agreement in place, your property distribution will be entirely determined by family law. You will be free to negotiate a settlement then with the knowledge of your exact financial position, or you can make an application to the court for orders (or even make a Financial Agreement after separation).

If you are the financially weaker party, it is usually the case that you will receive a greater distribution of property under family law than you would if a Financial Agreement was in place.

Financial Agreements set aside by the courts

The laws regarding Financial Agreements are quite complex and there are many situations where an agreement might be set aside by the courts. These include:

▶　　The agreement was obtained by fraud (including non-disclosure of a relevant matter).

▶　　Circumstances that have arisen since the agreement was made that make it impracticable for the agreement, or a part of the agreement, to be carried out.

▶　　There has been an important change in circumstances relating to a child of the relationship, resulting in hardship.

▶　　A party was engaged in unconscionable conduct at the time the agreement was made.

The law of contracts is applied when the courts consider Financial Agreements. Again, getting good legal advice is the best thing to do if you find yourself in circumstances where there is doubt about an agreement. Your lawyer will advise you about issues such as fraud, non-disclosure, duress and unconscionable conduct.

In some situations, one party is in a much stronger financial position and may insist on entering into a Financial Agreement at the beginning of a relationship or a marriage. It is very important that the financially stronger person does not exert undue pressure on the other to sign, because the agreement might later be declared null and void on the grounds of duress. If you feel under pressure in these circumstances, get your lawyer to write to the lawyer on the other side and place it on record that you feel you have no option but to sign the document – that you are in fact 'under duress'.

Specialist legal advice is essential if you want to maximise your chances of having a valid and binding Financial Agreement.

Save on stamp duty

The transfer of interests in property – which would normally be subject to stamp duty – is exempt where it is done under the terms of a Financial Agreement. This is so whether it is a Financial Agreement between a married or a de facto couple.

Stamp duty is normally not payable where the transfer of property is made under the provisions of the *Family Law Act*. This means that transfers by consent orders and orders made in contested proceedings will also be exempt.

IF IT POSITIVELY, DEFINITELY HAS TO GO TO COURT

SUMMARY

▶ Court proceedings usually take a long time, are expensive and can be emotionally exhausting. They can go on for years, not months or weeks.

▶ There are many stages to the court process – you don't just turn up one time and your case is over. There are several hearings and conferences to settle the matter on the way and before you get to the final trial.

▶ Did we say expensive? Going to court can be VERY EXPENSIVE. Depending on how far into the process it goes, it will cost in the tens of thousands and, in some cases, the legal fees are in the millions.

▶ Your lawyer should be able to give you an estimate of what your particular case will cost.

▶ Alternatively, you can run your own case in court and represent yourself. This may be difficult and time consuming and, if you don't get it right, there can be some pretty serious consequences.

Going to court

Litigation means going to court. This chapter explains the court process and provides some hints on how to deal with it.

Each of the courts that administer family law has an excellent website setting out their procedures, information, forms to download and 'how to' guides. Have a look at these sites because this book only provides a simplified version of the court system.

Most separations never reach the Family Courts. Many are resolved by the parties without ever seeing a lawyer – especially where there are few assets to 'divvy up' and the couple can resolve issues about the kids. However, sometimes you will end up in the Family Courts no matter how hard you try to avoid it. The many reasons why this may occur were discussed in earlier chapters.

Litigation is not pleasant and it can be a long and expensive process. It can also leave deep and lasting scars on you and on relationships with others.

In most Australian courts – including the Family Courts – the litigation process is adversarial, which means that each disputing party puts their opposing cases before the court. You put your best case forward and the other party does the same. It is inevitable that each side also paints the worst possible version of the other's case.

Family law gives judges and magistrates wide discretionary powers. Therefore, a win-lose result is uncommon (unlike contract or criminal law matters where it is always the case). In the Family Courts it is more likely that it will be a case of lose-lose, with neither of you ending up with everything you want. Both can end up worse off than if you had negotiated a settlement at the outset, especially after costs are taken into account.

We generally refer to the people involved in court proceedings as 'the parties'. This is the legal description of those on opposing sides. In family law, more than just ex-partners may be parties to the dispute. 'Third parties' might become involved where their interests are mixed up with the outcome of family law issues, for example, creditors, relations, a company or a trust. Sometimes, adult children might be involved in cases where they have a financial interest in the outcome of the dispute between their parents.

The court process simplified

The diagram 'Simplified court process' that follows below illustrates the basic court process, from the start of proceedings until final resolution by a judge. The diagram only provides a general guide, as there are variations in the different courts and between different registries (geographical branches) of courts.

Simplified court process

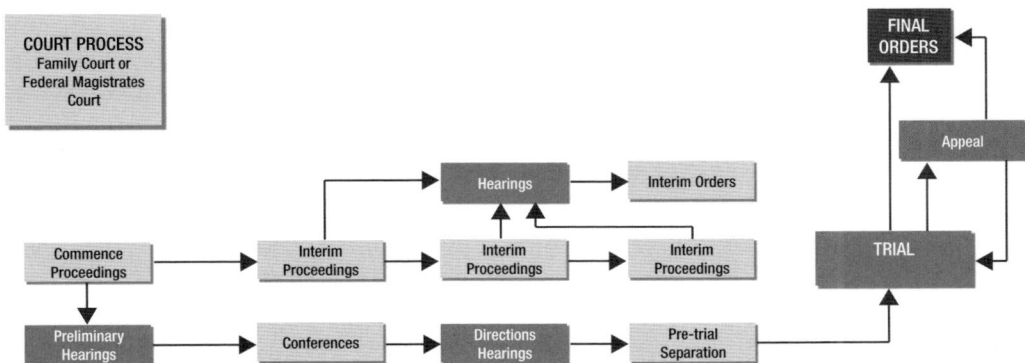

Across various courts and registries, the bottom line is basically the same:

▸ you start proceedings by asking the court to resolve the issues you cannot agree on

▸ you (and/or your lawyer) attend various conferences and hearings,

▸ you prepare for the final hearing

▸ you have a trial

▸ you get a decision, and

▸ your dispute is finalised.

Different courts, same laws

The courts that deal with family law matters are:

▸ the Family Court of Australia (FCA)

▸ the Federal Magistrates Court (FMC), and

▸ the Family Court of Western Australia (FCWA).

There are several registries of these courts and they also 'go on circuit'. Going on circuit is when officers of the court travel to locations throughout Australia where there is no Family Court building to deal with family law matters. In some areas, magistrates or local courts have the power to deal with some family law issues.

There is no Federal Magistrates Court in Western Australia. For practical purposes, the Family Court of Western Australia exercises all of the Federal powers under the *Family Law Act*. Although the building that houses the Family Court of Western Australia is located in Perth, court officials travel to population centres throughout Western Australia to hear family law matters and conduct conferences and hearings.

THE FEDERAL MAGISTRATES COURT

The majority of the work done in the Federal Magistrates Court (FMC) is in the area of family law. Although many types of orders can be made in the FMC, some can only be made in the Family Court – for example, those relating to validity of marriages and divorces.

Many matters will be heard initially in the FMC, as it has far more judicial officers available to hear cases and has authority to oversee most issues. However, if matters are particularly complex or deal with large sums of money, they will probably be heard in the Family Court.

Proposals to rationalise the structures of the Federal Magistrates Court and the Family Court of Australia have been around for some time. However, at the time of writing, this has not happened. So we have two courts exercising essentially the same powers throughout most of Australia.

Divorces are dealt with by the FMC. As a very general rule, the FMC also deals with less complex children and property matters. Where there is doubt, each court has the power to transfer matters to the other. Some issues can only be dealt with by the Family Court of Australia. If you are not sure where to go, have a look at the court websites or get specialised legal advice.

Interim issues

There are usually some 'interim proceedings' (sometimes referred to as an application in a case) to take care of issues that have to be resolved before the final hearing.

The range of possibilities for interim issues in children's and financial matters is almost endless. The issues could include, for example, short-term actions for children's living arrangements, whether someone should be stopped from accessing a bank account, whether you or your ex should be allowed exclusive use of the home, or whether someone should be compelled to sign passport applications for the children.

Further information is given about interim matters later in this chapter.

Jurisdiction – the courts' capacity to hear matters

Before you commence proceedings in the courts, you must ensure that the court has the jurisdiction to consider the issues. Practically speaking, this means that:

▸ The issues must be relevant to family law.

▸ The court has been given the power under the *Family Law Act* to determine these matters.

▸ You are a person who is allowed to start the court proceedings in question.

If, for example, you are seeking orders in relation to property issues, these must be covered by Part VIII of the *Family Law Act* (or some related legislation). If you have a dispute before you are separated, the Family Court will not entertain it. If you are in a relationship that is not 'de facto', as defined in the *Family Law Act,* you are in the wrong courts.

You must also:

- be present in Australia, or

- be ordinarily resident in Australia, or

- be an Australian citizen.

JURISDICTION OF THE FAMILY COURTS

If you have doubts about whether your issues should properly come before the Family Courts, or that you are permitted to bring them, you should go to the Family Court's website at:

www.familycourt.gov.au/wps/wcm/connect/FCOA/home/about/FCoA/AFL_Overview *or consult a family lawyer.*

The court process

You start proceedings by asking the court to resolve any issues you cannot agree on. You then attend various conferences and hearings, prepare for the final hearing, have a trial and get a decision. The matter is then concluded (unless either party appeals to a higher court).

The pathway towards, and once inside, the court usually unfolds as follows:

- You try to resolve matters (pre-action Process).

- You have compulsory mediation in children's matters (dispute resolution process).

- You file – or respond to – an application to the court (initiating application or response).

- A hearing or conference takes place in the court to assess the matter. At this point, directions or orders may be made by the court (case assessment conference or directions hearing).

- You attend a conference with the aim to get issues settled (conciliation conference).

- If issues are not settled, you prepare your matter for the trial.

> ▸ A further hearing may be held to determine your readiness for the trial (pre-trial conference, readiness conference or directions hearing).

> ▸ A trial is held before a judge (the trial).

> ▸ A judgment is issued by the court, finally resolving the issues you and your ex-partner brought before the court.

In between all of this, there might be exchanges of documents, experts' reports (especially if there are disputes over children's arrangements or property values), correspondence with the other side and further attempts at mediation or a negotiated settlement. Sometimes, the court will appoint an expert to investigate and report on issues involving children and may order the appointment of a lawyer to represent the children (called an Independent Children's Lawyer).

Interim issues (described earlier in this chapter) that have to be resolved before the final hearing will also be dealt with at various stages during the court process.

Pre-action procedures

Family Law Rules (which are not strictly binding in the Federal Magistrates Court) require you to make a formal effort to resolve matters before commencing proceedings in court. You should therefore:

> ▸ identify the issues that are in dispute

> ▸ propose the use of dispute resolution procedures other than going to court

> ▸ advise the other party of the settlement terms you are seeking, and

> ▸ in property matters:
>
> - provide details of financial documents in your possession, and
>
> - ask for copies of financial documents the other party may have.

In **all children's matters**, except in cases where there is violence or urgency, you must attend compulsory mediation with a registered organisation or registered family law dispute resolution practitioners and obtain a certificate of mediation before commencing proceedings. The requirement for a certificate is currently not necessary for property matters, but it has been proposed and may become law in future.

The pre-action procedures are not always followed, especially in property matters.

In some registries of courts, proceedings are commenced without each party having a clear idea of the issues in dispute and what it might take to get things settled. We recommend that you (or your lawyers, should you choose to use them) try to follow the procedures in the family law rules and request the other side do so as well. It may save a lot of unnecessary work and angst later in the process if you have a clear idea at the start of proceedings what issues need to be settled, rather than at the end.

Not everyone will co-operate, but it is better to demonstrate to the court that you have made every effort to resolve matters sensibly and fairly and it certainly cannot hurt your case to be clear about your proposals for settlement.

Offers to settle

Making an offer to settle disputes on realistic and reasonable terms has two effects: it improves the possibility of getting the conflict resolved early and it increases your chances of obtaining an order from the court that the other party should pay your legal costs.

When determining who should pay costs, a judge may take into account whether a party has made an offer in writing to settle the dispute or whether a party has been 'entirely successful' in the proceedings.

So, make a realistic offer to settle straight away. If your offer is rejected but you eventually get a result that is better or equal to your offer, you increase the chance of getting some of your costs paid by the other party.

An early offer to settle also puts pressure on the other party to consider whether it is worth spending heaps of money on legal fees when there is a risk of a costs order against them (which would mean they pay your costs as well as their own – a very expensive prospect).

Commencing proceedings – Application for Final Orders

Formal proceedings start with one person making an Application for Final Orders to the court. Links to court websites for these documents and how to process them are included in the box 'Guidelines for preparing and filing an initiating application' that follows on page 135.

In short, the application sets out your relevant details and states what orders you want the court to make. In financial matters, the application will be accompanied by a financial statement (which can also be obtained from the court websites). In some cases – and for all matters in the Federal Magistrates Court – affidavits (sworn statements of the facts you claim to be relevant to the dispute) also have to be prepared and filed with the Application for Final Orders.

GUIDELINES FOR PREPARING AND FILING AN INITIATING APPLICATION

Family Court of Australia
**www.familylawcourts.gov.au/wps/wcm/connect/FLC/Home/Forms/
Family+Law+Courts+forms/Initiating+Application**

Federal Magistrates Court
www.fmc.gov.au/forms/html/family_law.html

Family Court of Western Australia
www.familycourt.wa.gov.au/K/kits.aspx

The application and any accompanying documents are then 'filed' in the court, which means that at least three copies of all the correct documents have to be taken to the court. The court officers will then 'stamp' the documents to show this has been done and allocate a date for the preliminary hearing of the matter. They will keep one copy for the court records and give you back the other copies for yourself and for you to provide to the other party.

One copy of the stamped documents then have to be 'served' on (legally presented to) your ex-partner. The requirements of each court for 'service' are set out on their websites. It is important that you comply with the exact requirements if you wish your matter to proceed without delay in the courts.

Responses

If you are on the receiving end of an Application for Final Orders, you need to respond or you run the risk of the court making the orders the other party has asked for.

Depending on the issues and the court, you may also have to prepare a financial statement and an affidavit.

The processes for preparing, filing and serving your Response are virtually the same as that for the application. You tell the court and your ex-partner what orders you want the court to make by registering and serving your documents.

In the response, you set out which of the orders sought by the other party you are prepared to agree to and what orders you want the court to make.

For example:

▸ You may agree with the application that the property be divided between you equally, but you may wish to retain the home and pay out your ex-partner, rather than the other way around. Or,

▸ You might agree with the proposed property arrangements, but disagree with the proposals for the children's living arrangements.

If you complied with the pre-action procedures, you and your ex-partner should know all of this anyway.

Court fees

Don't forget the courts also charge fees at certain stages of the family law process. Find out what they are from the court website or ask your lawyer to provide the relevant information.

COURT FEES

To get up-to-date information on fees, check the website of the relevant court.

For example, the Federal Magistrates Court site can be found at:
www.fmc.gov.au/html/fees_family.html

Directions hearing

The first time you are likely to be required to attend the court is for the first hearing. The nature of the hearing will differ depending on which court you are in. In any event, the date and the address for the first hearing will be notified on the first page of the application and the response.

HEARING DATES

The court websites publish court lists each day. Check them or the newspapers to confirm that your matter is in the list and which court room will be used. This will save you time trying to locate where your matter is being heard when you get to court.

Family Court of Australia:
www.familylawcourts.gov.au/wps/wcm/connect/FLC/Home/Court%20Lists/

Family Court of Western Australia:
www.familycourt.wa.gov.au/D/daily_court_list.
aspx?uid=6114-4818-4955-6945

Federal Magistrates Court:
www.fmc.gov.au/lists/index.html

If there are interim issues to be heard, you should be prepared to argue the matter before the magistrate or give your lawyer all the information required to enable him or her to argue for you.

In some circumstances, your lawyer will engage a barrister to appear in court for you. Barristers are lawyers who specialise in court work and are often engaged when the issues to be argued in court are complex. Barristers may charge by an hourly rate – that is, on the basis of how much time they spend preparing for, and attending, the hearing of your matter. Many of them will ask that your lawyer also attend the hearing (so you end up paying for both to be there).

ATTENDANCE AT COURT HEARINGS AND CONFERENCES

Always check with the court about the requirement to attend the different hearings and conferences that may be scheduled. Ask your lawyer (if you have one). If in doubt, attend.

You are entitled to attend every hearing or conference that involves your case and you are required to attend most of them.

If you are representing yourself, you must attend every hearing or conference that is listed.

If you do not have a lawyer, you should have a very good knowledge of the matters included in your documents and the reasons for the orders you are seeking. The judge, registrar or magistrate will almost certainly ask you questions about them.

At the end of the first hearing – whether interim issues are involved or not – the court will make orders and/or directions about your matter. Take careful note of what has been decided. If you are in any doubt about what is required, or what has been ordered, ask the magistrate to clarify or explain matters to you.

Although the court orders will be printed out and sent to you (or your lawyer) after the hearing, it is always sensible to find out at the hearing what is proposed in case you have problems with complying. Otherwise, you may have to ask for another court date to try to undo what was done the first time. This is a waste of everyone's time and, often, your money.

The court orders will almost always specify when the matter will come before the court again.

COURT FORMALITIES AND PROCESSES

A word of warning: You must conform with the formalities in the court processes.

When in court:

▶ *Always treat the court officials with respect. They are just doing their job – which is often a difficult one.*

▶ *Try not to raise your voice or be argumentative. Never be abusive or insulting towards the other parties or their lawyers, no matter what they might say or do.*

▶ *Every time you appear in court, you are on show and you are creating an impression on the court. Put your best foot forward – present your arguments in a rational and clear way and be calm and controlled at all times.*

If you do not feel capable of presenting your arguments in a court room, which might be full of people, engage a lawyer to do it for you. That is their job and they should do it competently and in your best interests.

The other advantage of having a lawyer represent you in court is that they should know the processes that will enable your case to proceed as quickly and effectively as possible, including the possibility of seeking a costs order against parties that do not comply with the rules of court.

Conciliation conference

Conciliation Conferences are often ordered in the Family Courts. This is a compulsory conference in front of a court officer (who may be a registrar or magistrate). It is attended by the parties (and, where applicable, their legal advisers), with a view to trying again to get matters resolved.

Theoretically, all parties are required to have clearly defined the issues in dispute and, in property matters, exchanged all relevant financial documents before the conference takes place. Regrettably, this is not always the case and much time and money is wasted where cases are inadequately prepared and the proper processes have not been followed.

Be prepared. You must come prepared to state your case clearly and explain why you want the orders you are asking the court to make. Know your case (and the other party's case), make sure you have read the documents carefully and have specific proposals to get matters resolved or proposals that will move the case forward (such as further disclosure of financial documents or temporary arrangements for the children). The conference will be fairly informal and held in private rooms in the court building.

What is said at a conciliation conference is described as being 'without prejudice'. It can be a bit confusing, but 'without prejudice' is a legal description for comments and statements that may not be repeated in court (especially at the trial) and used against you. For example, if at the conference you offered to settle everything on a 50/50 basis just to get it resolved out of court, the other party cannot then repeat that to the judge at the trial where you might be seeking a 60/40 distribution in your favour.

Typically, a registrar will start off the conference by asking each party directly what their case is about and then look for ways to find a compromise. If you are represented by a lawyer, he or she may respond but you will always have the opportunity to say directly what you want (keeping in mind the cautions about how to behave in court set out in the box 'court formalities and processes' on page 139).

Sometimes, registrars will be very direct and tell you that they do not believe the court will make the orders you are seeking. Some will simply advise each of the parties to think carefully about the costs of what they are doing, suggest that no one will get exactly what they want and point out that there are no guarantees in the court process. They might make comments such as:

"You must consider the costs that are involved in this and realise that, although you both have lawyers who deserve to be properly paid for what they do, it is your hard-earned money that is going into their pockets at the end of the day ... and I am sure they would both much prefer that it be settled and that we can get some orders done today and finalise the matter."

After consideration of the issues, the registrar may adjourn the conference and request that the parties leave the room to see whether they can resolve the matter and return with some draft orders.

If you have managed to make progress, many of the registrars will continue the conference to try to bring your positions closer together in the hope of achieving a resolution. Sometimes this happens, sometimes not. If matters can be resolved at this stage – whether entirely or in part – orders will be made by the registrar on the basis of what you have agreed and those issues will then be finalised.

Anything that is not resolved will proceed to the next stage, in preparation for a trial before a judge. In these circumstances, the registrar will make further orders regarding what needs to be done to prepare for a trial.

Listing (directions) hearing

In many cases the court will 'list the matter' (call it back for a further hearing) to assess whether it is ready to proceed to the final trial. Again, you will be advised of the date and place for the hearing and, unless represented by a lawyer, you would be required to attend at that time.

This is usually the final court event before the trial is held. Depending on the court, this event may be a conference (in private and 'without prejudice') or a hearing in open court. Some judges actually include this as part of the trial process, so that everything that is said forms part of the evidence upon which he or she makes a final decision.

This final pre-trial event can be called a pre-trial conference, but may also be called a readiness conference or a directions hearing.

Essentially, the court wants to be satisfied that all is in readiness for the trial and that no issues or matters are outstanding that might interfere with the proper conduct of the trial. If you are not prepared, the court may delay the trial and order that you pay any costs of delay. So, make sure that you have done everything you are required to do to start the trial – disclosing documents, obtaining valuations, having your witnesses ready to appear and similar preparatory issues.

When all is in readiness, the court will set a trial date and allocate the time required to hear all the evidence. This may be a day or it may be weeks. That will depend on the issues that are to be argued, the number of witnesses, the evidence that is to be presented and similar issues.

The aim is to get all the matters heard at one time, to allow the judge to then make a fully informed decision on all issues.

Trial

The trial is your opportunity to present the evidence in support of the orders you want the judge to make and tell the judge why those orders should be made.

Once all of the evidence has been given by all of the parties, the judge will be able to make a decision that deals with all of the issues in dispute.

This is the last opportunity you will get, so make sure you get it right and present the best case you can.

PRESENTING YOUR CASE AT TRIAL

Think carefully about going to trial without getting legal advice.
At the trial, you may have to make submissions to the court based on family law and its application to parts of, or to all of, the case you are putting forward.

Therefore, if you are not represented by a lawyer at this stage, you could be at a significant disadvantage.

The court will give you every opportunity to put forward your case. However, the judge will not make your case for you or assist you to present the proper legal basis for your case.

Preparing the case for trial

The three rules of buying real estate are 'Location, location and location'. The rule of three also applies to getting ready for a trial, where it becomes 'Preparation, preparation and preparation'.

Affidavits

Your primary evidence at the trial is given by affidavit. This is a written statement setting out the facts of your case. Affidavits are sworn under oath or affirmed as to the truth of their contents. They are the written equivalent of the evidence that you give verbally when you appear in court: 'the truth, the whole truth and nothing but the truth'.

A separate affidavit is usually required from each of the parties and from every witness who will be called in support of the respective cases.

Preparation of these affidavits is one of the most important aspects of your whole case. It is the primary evidence you are putting before the court to enable the judge to make a decision in your favour. Preparing good affidavits requires skill and care and can be very time consuming. All of the relevant issues have to be covered and all of the facts have to be stated accurately. Irrelevant information (no matter how emotionally attached you may be to it) has to be avoided. Argument is not permissible – you are not making your argument in your affidavit but simply stating the facts that are relevant to the case you are putting to the judge. Arguments made in an affidavit will be ignored and will probably only irritate the judge who has to read them.

The length of your trial affidavit is not the key. The really important issue is presenting in a coherent and logical way those facts that are really relevant to the outcome you seek. Including anything else in your affidavit is not evidence.

You must consider the position you intend to put forward at the trial and what evidence supports that case or undermines the case of the other party. So, you have to work backwards – start with the result you want and then work back to what you have to prove in order to support that result.

For example, if you want the judge to give you a greater share of the asset pool than the other person, work out what legal principles support that conclusion (such as a greater contribution at the start of the relationship) and then set out the facts upon which you rely (such as evidence of assets you had before the relationship began). Remember the '1, 2, 3 of property' in chapter 4? It won't help you to tell the court how the other party did nothing around the house for years unless you can give evidence about your own contributions. It won't help to say in your affidavit that you deserve more than the other party simply because you are a more committed or hard-working person.

There is a real skill in preparing good affidavits; following a logical and methodical process will be more likely to convince the judge than just blurting it all out.

If you are seeking orders that the children spend more time with you than the other party, make sure you are armed with the evidence required by the *Family Law Act* that shows this would be in the children's best interests. It will not help your case that your evidence is simply your honestly-held opinion that they would be better off with you. It is unhelpful to say simply that you think you are the best-placed parent to have the children live with you without supporting evidence – facts. You must demonstrate **why** this is so. The best way to do this is to look at what the judge has to consider and then set out the facts that demonstrate your situation meets these requirements.

Remember: simply saying that something is true does not make it true. Nor does it provide the basis of credible evidence in the courts. You must provide cold, hard evidence in support of your position and the evidence must be relevant under family law.

EVIDENCE MUST BE RELEVANT

In a recent case in the Family Court in Melbourne, a party in a financial matter thought he had 'covered all of the bases' by filing an affidavit that overflowed three lever-arch files – hundreds of pages. He was not represented by a lawyer and thought all of this material would help his case.

At the hearing prior to the trial, the judge considered the material and deleted 188 paragraphs of the affidavit (almost the whole document) on the grounds that it could not be used as evidence at the trial because it was irrelevant, argumentative and simply a statement of opinion.

The husband was left with virtually no evidence in support of his case. In addition to this setback, compelling the judge to go through the affidavit paragraph by paragraph did little for goodwill – the judge was clearly frustrated by the irrelevance of the information.

This can also happen during the trial itself if you attempt to put documents or 'evidence' before the court that does not comply with the rules of evidence.

Evidence may only be put before a court in accordance with the rules of law. Some of these rules can be a bit confusing. For example, the rules relating to 'hearsay' evidence mean that you cannot put to a court something that you have heard someone else say to establish the truth of your comment. What you are saying might be perfectly true but that does not necessarily mean it is acceptable as evidence in a court.

This is where lawyers really come into their own – helping you gather and present evidence that is 'admissible', or allowable, in court. They usually know what is relevant and supports your case, and the best way to present the arguments.

Preparing for the hearing

Preparing for court hearings requires planning for what lies ahead. Here are some things you could do to make sure that you are properly prepared:

- ▶ Ask your lawyer for copies of all of the documents.

- ▶ Make sure you understand the evidence you will give and that you have read and re-read all of the affidavits that you have provided.

- ▶ Check whether or not you will be expected to give evidence.

- ▶ Make sure you meet your barrister before the hearing to talk over the matter.

- ▶ It's often a good idea to visit the court building in the days ahead of the hearing to watch some proceedings and to get a feel for what happens in court.

- ▶ Listen carefully to your lawyer's advice about the proper way to give evidence and to answer questions in court. Generally, the formula is to answer questions directly and simply, without going into lengthy explanations. Most questions simply require "yes", "no" or "I don't know".

What happens in court?

Finally, the day has arrived

By now, you will have been prepared to attend the court. How you dress should show respect for the court. Suits, even jackets, are not necessary in the Family Courts. On the other hand, dirty clothes, work clothes or ripped jeans with thongs are unlikely to endear you to the judge – even if you intend to show how hard-working or impoverished you are. Dress neatly and comfortably in smart casual clothing.

Your lawyer will be wearing a suit and sometimes legal robes.

The Family Court room

The court room for a family law matter will look something like this:

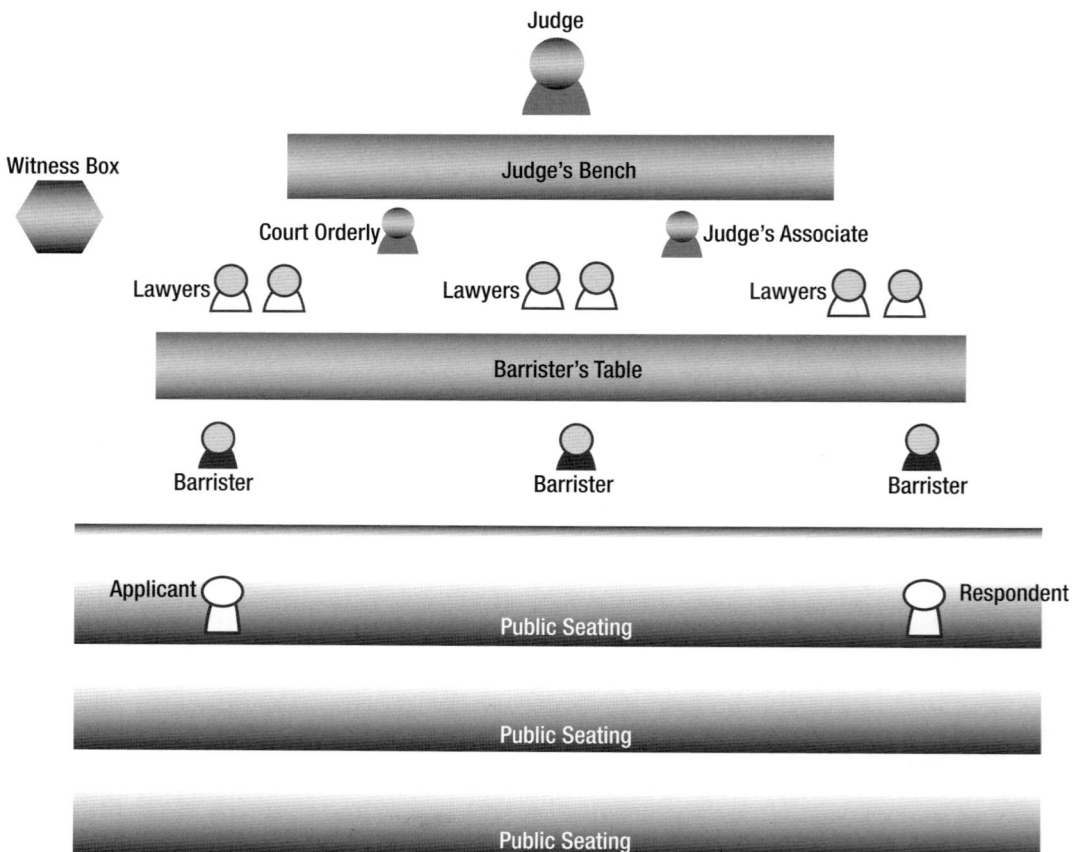

Judge

Witness Box

Judge's Bench

Court Orderly

Judge's Associate

Lawyers

Lawyers

Lawyers

Barrister's Table

Barrister

Barrister

Barrister

Applicant

Respondent

Public Seating

Public Seating

Public Seating

Attend the court well ahead of the hearing time so that you can discuss any last-minute issues with your lawyers and get the feel of the court room where your case is being heard. Check and re-check the hearing time and also the location of the court.

Children under the age of 18 are not permitted in court, however there are child-minding facilities in many registries. You may want to check ahead of time what services are available for minding your children so that you are prepared if you have to bring them with you.

Witnesses who will be giving evidence in the case are not allowed into the court room until they have been called as a witness or have been specifically permitted to attend by the judge. The parties are entitled to be present in court throughout the hearing.

It is usually best not to bring new partners to hearings unless they are to give evidence. Creating tension with your ex-partner achieves nothing.

As illustrated in the diagram on the previous page, depending on whether you are the applicant or the respondent, you will sit in the court in the public gallery immediately behind the table occupied by your legal team. If in doubt, your lawyer will show you where to sit. Unlike American court dramas, the lawyers do not stroll around the court room while making statements or questioning witnesses, but address the court from behind their tables.

When called, witnesses sit in the box at the front of the court room where they can be seen by the judge and are close to whoever might be questioning them.

The trial itself

At the trial, each party presents their case to the court in a controlled way. The judge presiding over the trial has a broad discretion as to how the proceedings will be conducted, subject to the requirements of family law and the rules of evidence that apply to that court.

Throughout much of the hearing, you will hear the parties referred to as 'the applicant' and 'the respondent'. If you commenced the legal proceedings, you will be the applicant. Otherwise, you are the respondent. There may be more than one respondent if third parties have been included in the proceedings (by their own choice or because one of the parties has included them). In almost all cases, the applicant presents his or her case first and, when this process is complete, the respondent presents their case.

Each party's primary evidence is presented by the affidavits that have already been filed in the court and copied to all parties. So, in theory at least, you cannot surprise the other party with a last-minute disclosure of something unknown.

A trial is usually opened by the applicant's barrister presenting an outline of the case (the opening).Then the applicant enters the witness box for questioning by the other party (or, more usually, the other party's barrister). Then each of the applicant's witnesses (who have provided affidavits and whose evidence the other side wants to question) will be called and sworn in to the witness box.

Each party may have filed several affidavits (in addition to their own), sworn by witnesses who are providing further factual evidence in support of the case. Every person who has provided an affidavit is required to appear in court if called by the other side and will then be questioned about the contents of their affidavit. If a witness fails to appear when called, the contents of the affidavit may be disregarded by the judge (and, if they have been subpoenaed to appear, they may be punished by the judge and can even be arrested). Questioning is usually conducted by the barrister representing the other side and is called cross examination. Barristers are usually very skilled and can make a terrible mess of a person's evidence and credibility if it is not accurate and truthful.

IF THE SUIT FITS

A senior family law barrister once compared an untruthful witness to a beautifully tailored Armani suit with just a single thread hanging from a sleeve.

The suit may look magnificent but the hanging thread is the untruth being put to the court. Pull that thread and the suit gradually unravels, leaving the witness in the witness box without the aura created by the stylish suit.

A skilful barrister can pull a whole case apart by exposing and working on a single lie. Cases can then unravel completely, just like the Armani suit.

Where your barrister and lawyers sit depends on the particular court you are in. There are different arrangements in different courts.

No matter how you feel about matters that are discussed during the trial, do your best not to react to what is said by a witness or the lawyer (or, especially, the judge). You may think what is being said is incorrect or deliberately misleading but it is up to your legal team, not you, to deal with what arises in the trial process. Even though it may be hard not to react, you should simply listen. If you don't understand what has happened, ask your lawyer to explain.

If something is said that is untruthful, and this point has not previously been discussed with your legal team (and is of significance and importance), make a note and let your lawyer know. If you are running your own case, raise the matter in cross examination of the relevant witness or mention the fact in your address to the judge.

Giving evidence

For most hearings in the Family Courts, you will not be required to enter the witness box to give verbal evidence. However, you will be required to do so if the matter goes to a trial.

Sitting in a witness box and giving evidence is a frightening thought for most of us. Most of us have never had to do it before.

You will be apprehensive about how your evidence might be received by the judge, concerned whether your lawyer will correct any of your mistakes and be terrified about the barrister's cross examination you are about to go through. Try to remain calm and focused.

When you are called to give evidence

You don't have to state again to the court all of what's said in your affidavit, as the judge will have read that document (and all the other affidavits submitted) and will already know what you claim to be the truth.

After you step into the witness box, you will be asked to swear or affirm that your evidence will be truthful. In most cases, your lawyer will then 'tidy up' any loose ends in your affidavit. They may clarify some elements that are not clear, adjust a statement that might not be entirely accurate or update information that has come to hand after the affidavit was made.

Then the other party's lawyer will question ('cross examine') you about what is in your affidavit and any other part of the case that is being considered by the court. This questioning can be very wide ranging and is likely to be quite detailed. Sometimes, the questioning can go on for many hours (even days). The following points might help:

▸ If you need a break, ask the judge to call one.

▸ Try to stay composed and alert to what is being asked.

▸ Do not lose your cool. It does not help your case to get into an argument with the barrister (who, after all, is just doing his or her job).

▸ If you can, relax, even when the barrister is trying to pick holes in your evidence. If you have told the truth in your affidavit, you have nothing to be concerned about.

▸ Focus on the questions and answer them in a straightforward and direct way.

▸ Do not go into detail unless you are specifically asked to do so.

▸ If a "yes" or "no" is required, just give that answer and no more.

▸ Do not try to 'out-think' the barrister and second-guess what he or she is trying to find out.

▸ Reply to the questions as you understand them. If you do not fully understand a question, ask the barrister to explain or to ask it again.

During your cross examination, there may be occasions when your lawyer stands up and interrupts the questioning. This will happen if your lawyer believes the questioning is not appropriate for some reason. When this happens, do not get involved, unless asked to by the judge. Simply wait until the judge sorts things out. In some circumstances, the judge will ask you to leave the court while he or she deals with a legal issue that might have arisen. This might happen, for example, if the judge considers you should not be allowed to hear the arguments because it might affect your evidence.

The judge may ask you questions from time to time as well. Listen carefully and, as with all questions put to you, answer directly and honestly.

When the other party's lawyer has finished questioning you, your own lawyer may ask you a few further questions (called 're-examination') to clarify aspects of the evidence.

When that is finished, your evidence to the court is over and the judge will excuse you from the witness box. You will not have to return to give further evidence (except in exceptional circumstances).

Telling the truth in court

Telling lies in court proceedings – whether it is what you put in your affidavit or what you say when giving evidence in the witness box – is called 'perjury'. Perjury is a criminal offence and can result in imprisonment.

While jail terms are not usual, telling untruths in the Family Courts has other consequences. The most obvious is that your credibility is damaged and, as a result, all of your evidence comes into question. This may result in your case falling apart, simply because your evidence is not believed the other person's version of the facts is preferred.

You should stick to the facts when giving evidence. Don't embellish the story by adding bits that aren't true.

Tell the whole truth. Don't try to hide or avoid parts of the evidence that might not do you great credit. No one is perfect and we have all made many mistakes in life. judges understand this. They are not there to judge your character or moral behaviour – they are making determinations under the *Family Law Act*. The weak spots in your case will have to be dealt with, just as much as the highlights.

TELL THE TRUTH – IT CAN BE EXPENSIVE IF YOU DON'T

In a lengthy trial in the Family Court, the wife was determined that the court would hear only her version of the facts, which required that she stray from the truth on more than one occasion.

Her evidence was so unbelievable and untrue that, when the judge issued his 100+ pages of reasons for judgment, he was not prepared to accept even one part of the wife's case – wherever her version differed from the husband's, the judge preferred the husband's, simply because the wife's credibility had been destroyed.

The second consequence was almost inevitable – the judge also ordered costs against the wife on an 'indemnity basis', meaning that she had to pay all of the fees that the husband had paid his lawyers – about $400,000 – on top of her own legal costs.

After all the applicant's witnesses have been called, the same happens with the Respondent and his or her witnesses, who will be cross examined by the applicant's lawyer.

When the respondent's witnesses have each had their stint in the witness box, each party closes its case. They do this by presenting submissions to the judge about the evidence, the law and the conclusions they want the judge to make as a result of what has been revealed at the trial.

You may be at a significant disadvantage presenting your final submission if you do not have a firm grasp of family law and the relevant rules of evidence. That is why parties are usually represented by lawyers (usually a lawyer and a barrister) in matters that go to trial.

When the trial is over

After the trial has concluded, you wait for the judge to make a decision.

Sometimes the judge will make final orders as soon as the parties have concluded final presentations. Reasons for the decision may be given immediately or at a later time.

One well-respected and now retired judge was in the habit of giving his decision and detailed reasons immediately after final presentations were over, having progressively written his judgment as the trial proceeded. Most of his judgments had the same ring about them, as he seemed to follow a well-worn template. But it was swift justice and no one was kept long in suspense.

In most matters, a judge will adjourn the matter for a decision to be delivered at some stage in the future – often some months later. The Family Court aims to have its judgments delivered within three months of the conclusion of the evidence but in some cases decisions have not been made for much longer.

Final orders

The end of the court process is the issuing of orders by the judge. This is when you are told what the judge has decided and what he or she determines is to happen with financial distribution and/or arrangements for your children. That's it. No arguments, unless you want to appeal (and that is another costly and lengthy process).

How long will it all take?

The court process can take a long time from start to finish. If your matter is not unduly complex and goes through all the steps to trial, it is unlikely that it will be over within nine months in the Federal Magistrates Court (and much longer in the Family Court). It may be a lot longer, depending on the court you are in and how many other matters are in the court list at the same time.

But most matters will settle earlier and not go all the way through the process to a trial, as shown in the following chart.

Settlement rates in the Federal Magistrates Court

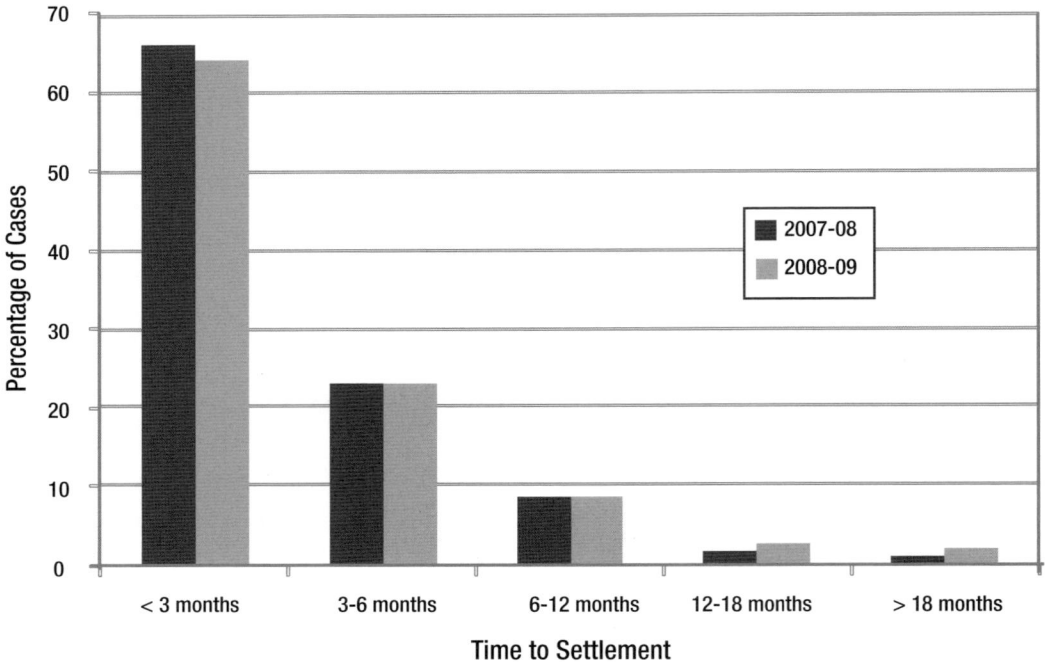

If your matter is complex, there is no saying how long it will take but, again, it will be much longer than the estimates above.

It will take six weeks or so from the time you make your first application to the first court hearing or conference.

At each court event, you will be advised when the next court event is likely to be, but don't be surprised if there are adjournments or delays along the pathway. Your lawyer should be able to give you updates and estimates as the matter progresses, but there is no guarantee that the court will be able to dispose of all the matters that are listed and when they are scheduled.

A defended trial in the Family Court may not be listed for several years after the matter has started. Patience may be necessary.

Getting off the court treadmill

Don't despair. You can settle your matter at any time – even if the trial has started.

Being involved in litigation does not put you on a treadmill that you can never get off. You can settle with your ex-partner at any time during the litigation process. In fact, roughly 90 per cent of cases are resolved before trial, and a further 5 per cent, or so, after a trial starts but before the judge has to make a decision.

So, if you end up in court, be alert to the possibility of getting your matter resolved as soon as possible by a sensible and pragmatic compromise. The longer you go on, the more it will cost and the more impact on involved parties – not to mention the collateral damage to kids, extended family and friends.

Keep trying to get your differences settled. You can apply to the court to make consent orders at any stage in the proceedings.

Complying with court orders

Once an order has been made by the court, it is legally binding and you must follow it.

There are penalties and sanctions for failing to comply with court orders. If you do not follow orders, you also leave yourself open to potential Costs orders against you, which may run to thousands of dollars.

The court does not look kindly on those who take the law into their own hands, so you would be well advised to read court orders carefully. If you do not understand them or are unsure about their full meaning, ask the judge to explain or seek legal advice about your responsibilities.

MOST MATTERS SETTLE

This graph shows how many matters settle even after court proceedings have commenced. Between lodging an application in the Family Court and final orders (judgment), about 90 per cent of cases settle.

Attrition Rates – Family Court of Australia

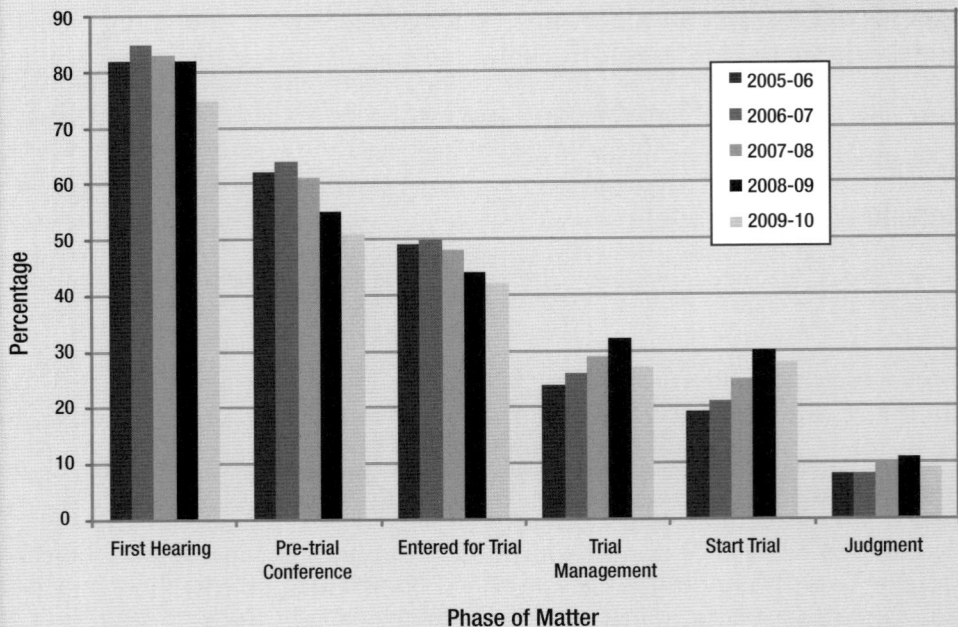

Bar chart legend:
- 2005-06
- 2006-07
- 2007-08
- 2008-09
- 2009-10

Y-axis: Percentage (0 to 90)
X-axis (Phase of Matter): First Hearing, Pre-trial Conference, Entered for Trial, Trial Management, Start Trial, Judgment

Source: Family Court of Australia Annual Report 2009-10

Children
It has been estimated that over 80 per cent of separated parents are able to make arrangements for their children through discussion and without the assistance of mediation. A further 6 per cent resolve arrangements through mediation or counselling. Only 10 per cent of all separated couples work out children's arrangements with a lawyer or through the Family Court system.

LAWYERS – FINDING THE RIGHT ONES AND WORKING WITH THEM

SUMMARY

▶ Over 80 per cent of people involved in the Family Court engage a lawyer to assist them. Many others use lawyers just for advice or to prepare documents.

▶ You should always do the cost-benefit analysis of hiring a lawyer against representing yourself – think about what you are paying for, why and what you expect to get out of it.

▶ Some lawyers who practice in family law are accredited specialists. This qualification means they have extra expertise and knowledge.

▶ If you engage a lawyer, you will probably have to sign a Legal Costs Agreement; the terms of this agreement determine your financial obligations to the lawyer.

▶ It is worth looking carefully at the agreement and understanding what you are going to be charged for and when you will be expected to pay.

▶ If you are not happy with your lawyer, you can change and, in some circumstances, you should consider a formal complaint about their conduct.

▶ You can do your own family law matter – if you know what you are doing.

Whether or not to engage a lawyer in a family law matter is simply a question of cost (and whether you are prepared to set aside the time to do it yourself). Do the benefits of having a lawyer justify spending the sort of money that is required for their services?

You should undertake this simple cost-benefit analysis when making the decision. If this analysis does not stack up, then you may as well do it yourself and save the money.

Remember to distinguish between legal advice and legal representation. You may need to obtain advice on the legal issues involved and how to deal with them but still be able to represent yourself in negotiations and in the court process.

You can only do the analysis accurately if you understand both sides of the equation: the costs and the benefits. So, here are some pretty basic questions:

- How important (or complicated) are the issues?
- Am I able to do what needs to be done without legal advice or representation at all?
- How much legal advice do I need?
- Do I really need a lawyer to represent me?
- How much will this cost me in lawyers' fees?
- What additional costs or fees might I incur and what might they be for?

Another way to look at the cost-benefit analysis might be as follows:

Costs

- How much does my lawyer propose to charge me? What is the top and bottom of the range of costs that I will have to pay?
- Is the lawyer prepared to guarantee how much the costs will be before starting work?
- What results can the lawyer guarantee me for this outlay?

Benefits

▸ What legal advice do I need that I can't find out myself?

▸ When do I need this advice?

▸ What risks do I face if I don't have that advice?

- Will I know all the options available to me to move forward?

- Am I likely to get my matter resolved faster with a lawyer? Is the speed of resolution important for me?

- Do I know how to finalise my matter in a legal way?

▸ Is representation by a lawyer necessary in my case? If so, what benefits will this representation provide?

▸ What are the risks of not being represented?

- Am I likely to be overwhelmed by the work involved?

- Will it put me at a disadvantage if the other party is represented and I am not?

- Will the matter take a lot longer if I do it myself?

You can do your own cost-benefit analysis by holding the answers to these questions against the likely fees and expenses.

Do you really need a lawyer?

Do you really need a lawyer for family law matters?

Most people who are involved in family law disputes would say that they are better off with a lawyer than without one. It's not much different to building a house. You are likely to be better off engaging a builder than doing it yourself.

There are three stages when you might think about engaging a lawyer:

▸ when you have separated (or are contemplating settlement)

▸ if you are trying to get issues settled and finalised without going to court, and

▸ if you have to go to court.

Advice at separation

If you are thinking about separating or have recently separated, getting some sound legal advice is usually a good thing to do. Initially, you may not even need a lawyer if there are no issues over children or property – although the cost of a preliminary meeting with a lawyer may be well worth the investment.

You are unlikely to be aware of your rights and responsibilities unless you have a pretty good knowledge of family law. Initially, you would only spend a minimal amount of money to get professional guidance about where you stand and the best way to move forward. Perhaps get a couple of legal opinions. You are not making a commitment to a long-term relationship with any lawyer at this stage – rather, you are simply finding out the best way to handle the situation.

At this stage it's really a no-brainer. If there are few issues over children or property you may not need to engage a lawyer to represent you, but the fees you pay for a preliminary meeting are likely to be worth it in the end.

Lawyers in the settlement process

As we have said throughout this book, it is in everyone's best interests to resolve disputes as quickly as possible. Getting your matter settled as early as possible saves you time, uncertainty, stress and legal expense.

Especially if you and your ex-partner have agreed the basic terms of your settlement, it can make good sense to have a lawyer prepare the agreement in the proper legal form and get it registered in court. Lawyers know what is required in the content of the agreement and the processes required for it to be formalised. They will also be able to tell you whether the proposed terms of settlement are fair and reasonable, or whether you are giving away far too much.

At this stage, a lawyer should be able to provide a fairly accurate estimate (if not an actual and fixed quote) of what it will cost to prepare the settlement documents. However, beware any estimate with a significant difference between the upper and lower limits.

It is also not unusual at this stage for a lawyer to tell you that you may be entitled to much more under family law. If that happens:

> ▸ Ask the lawyer to confirm their advice about your entitlements in writing.

▶ Ask how much it will cost to take matters further and how much time it will take (also in writing, please).

▶ Work out whether it makes good economic sense to incur these additional costs (take the lawyer's top estimate) against their lowest estimate of what you stand to gain.

You then need to balance the likely financial costs against the probable consequences of not settling, including the cost in time, stress and the impact of ongoing conflict on everyone involved.

If you are asking for consent orders, the court has to be satisfied that the settlement proposal is fair and reasonable and otherwise meets the requirements of the *Family Law Act*. If the proposal you brought to the table is unreasonable, the court will probably reject the consent orders.

If you decide to settle, read on.

If not, skip forward to 'Lawyers in the litigation (court) process' on page 162.

Time

It will probably be quicker if you have a lawyer to do the paperwork for a settlement. They know the process and what has to be done to get matters finalised. A competent lawyer should know what to put in the agreement and what to leave out. Most of them have done this before and should be able to process your instructions quickly and efficiently.

▶ If in doubt, ask the lawyer how long it will take to finalise everything (get a commitment), and

▶ If you are not satisfied that everything will be handled promptly, go to another lawyer.

Certainty

All agreements over property or children should be in writing and either formalised by a court or prepared as a Financial Agreement. Otherwise, your agreement is not binding or enforceable.

A lawyer can draft your agreement in the right terms and make sure that all of the loose ends are tied up, so that making the consent orders will finalise your matter once and for all. This will give you the certainty that you won't have to deal with these issues again.

If you are attempting to do it yourself, there may be a nagging feeling that not everything has been ticked off (and what the consequences of that failure might be).

Stress

Engaging a lawyer to draft up your settlement documents – and perhaps to negotiate any lingering unresolved issues – allows you to leave these worries in their hands. The lawyer should be able to resolve these matters objectively and in accordance with your instructions, relieving you of much of the stress you would otherwise face at this time.

Cost

If costs are reasonable and proportionate to the issues and the values involved, paying for a lawyer's skills at this stage is likely to be a realistic and fair investment for you. It might save a major court battle in the event matters are not properly dealt with in the first place or finalised according to the law.

Again, it comes back to the question of what your lawyer proposes to charge for the services provided. You may find some lawyers are simply too expensive, as their hourly rates are comparatively high, relative to the job that you want them to do. At the end of the day, you are paying the money, so you must be satisfied that their services are worth it.

Lawyers in the litigation (court) process

It has been estimated that family law 'market' generates $1.6 billion in lawyers' fees each year. (This statistic does not even include the costs of barristers).

The cost of proceedings in any of the Family Courts can be very expensive. A Sydney newspaper article recently put the average cost of a family law case at $40,000 – for **each** party, not the combined cost! Some large cases take many years to work their way through the court system and cost each side millions of dollars in legal fees.

Your decision to engage a lawyer has major financial consequences, so it is not to be taken lightly.

Most people whose matters end up in court do engage lawyers. There are some pretty obvious reasons for this:

▶ The court processes are complicated and demanding (lawyers are trained to deal with this).

▶ Appearing in court and presenting your own case is a daunting task – especially if the other party has a lawyer who knows the ropes.

▶ A lawyer can advise you about legally realistic alternatives.

▶ A lawyer can help you avoid the possible consequences of adverse costs orders.

LAWYERS IN THE FAMILY COURTS

Most people have lawyers:
Between 80-85 per cent of all parties in the Family Courts have lawyers to represent them.

In the Family Court
▶ *Lawyers represented both parties in about three quarters of matters in the Family Court.*
▶ *In about 20 per cent of cases, only one party had a lawyer.*
▶ *Neither person had a lawyer in only around 10 per cent of cases.*

In the Federal Magistrates Court
▶ *About two-thirds of cases had lawyers on both sides.*
▶ *Almost 30 per cent of cases had lawyers on one side only.*
▶ *The percentage of 'non-lawyer' cases was less than 10 per cent.*

The benefits of having competent representation and advice are pretty clear. However, you should ask yourself whether the results you anticipate will justify that cost.

Insurance against bad lawyers

There is no guarantee that a lawyer will handle your matter competently and effectively. Despite the efforts of the regulatory bodies to ensure that lawyers maintain very high professional and ethical standards, there are bad apples in every barrel. However, if your lawyer makes a complete mess of your case, you may be able to take further action.

Firstly, you can lodge a complaint about a lawyer's behaviour with the regulatory body in your state. Complaints may be about overcharging, failure to follow instructions, improper conduct, etc. Your complaints will be investigated and your lawyer's handling of the matter examined, possibly resulting in serious consequences. Other ways of dealing with disputes over your lawyer's costs are covered later in this chapter under 'Not happy with your lawyer?' on page 177.

You may be able to take action against your lawyer to recover any damages you may have incurred due to their failure to deal properly with your matter. For example, if your lawyer fails to draft appropriate orders to finalise your matter and you suffer losses as a result, the lawyer may be liable to you for damages as a result of their negligence.

This is a last resort and obviously not a situation you would wish to be in – but it might be better than having made a mess of it without a lawyer.

Choosing a lawyer

So, you have decided that it is probably in your best interests to have a lawyer. How to find the right one?

In view of the importance of the issues at stake, this is a pretty important decision and it is likely to have a significant impact on at least the next few months of your life.

Many people find their lawyer through the recommendation of a friend, a colleague or their accountant or doctor. Others look up the Yellow Pages or contact the Law Society or Law Institute in their state for a list of family law practitioners.

Whichever method you choose, prepare a shortlist, then make an appointment and talk to those on your list.

You should also determine up front whether you want to get matters resolved as quickly and cheaply as possible (but fairly for all parties), or whether you are spoiling for a fight, which might take a long time and cost a lot of money. No-one can deny you your 'day in court', if that's what you are after. However, think about the consequences before you commit to that course of action. Whatever you decide will have a bearing on the kind of lawyer that you select.

Your first consultation with a lawyer does not mean that you are committed to that lawyer for the entire period of your family law matter, or even at all. If you engage a lawyer and start working with them, you can pay the bill at any time and switch to another lawyer (or handle the matter yourself).

Consider also at this stage whether you need a specialist family lawyer or whether you want a lawyer who engages in 'collaborative law'.

Specialist lawyers – there is a difference

In some areas of law – including family law – a number of lawyers with special knowledge and expertise are qualified as accredited specialists. Generally, these lawyers indicate their specialist status by using a logo similar to the one in the box 'Accredited Family Law Specialists' that follows on page 166.

A Family Law Accredited Specialist must be a lawyer who has a substantial family law practice, has passed intensive examination and skills testing and maintains their professional qualifications by attending appropriate training each year. Each specialist has worked in family law for at least five years.

In a sense, a specialist in any area of law is similar to a specialist medical practitioner. If you have skin problems you would see a dermatologist, a pediatrician looks after children, if your eyes are playing up you might be referred to an ophthalmologist. So, if your legal issues are in relation to family law and you want some really expert advice, it makes sense to go to a specialist family lawyer. Like medical specialists, they can cost more, but this is not necessarily the case. In any event, you may feel the extra expertise is worth the extra expense.

ACCREDITED FAMILY LAW SPECIALISTS

The accredited specialist logo looks similar to this in every state.

If you want to find an Accredited Family Law Specialist, contact the relevant legal organisation in your state:

Victoria
www.liv.asn.au/Specialists

New South Wales
www.lawsociety.com.au/community/findingalawyer/findalawyersearch/ index.htm

Queensland
www.qls.com.au

Western Australia
www.lawsocietywa.asn.au/accredited-family-law-specialists

South Australia
www.lawsocietysa.asn.au/pdf/SAAccreditedSpecialists.pdf

Collaborative law

Collaborative law is a model originally developed in the USA about 20 years ago. It is also available in Canada and the UK. More recently it has found its way to Australia and New Zealand.

What is collaborative law?

In recent years, a growing number of lawyers have been practising collaborative law in Australia. This is a negotiation model where lawyers and their clients sign an agreement to work together to resolve a dispute without court involvement. The stated aim is to reach agreement while minimising costs, delays and stress.

Theoretically, this process aligns your lawyer's interests with yours as the client, as both you and your lawyers want to get the dispute settled.

If required, financial advisers, accountants or valuers may also be brought into the negotiations.

Under collaborative law, lawyers must cease their involvement if the negotiations fail to produce an agreement; they are not permitted to act for their clients in any later court process. If the process is unsuccessful, both sides must find new lawyers and start from scratch – and this would come at a financial and time cost.

Under collaborative law, the discussions and negotiations are 'without prejudice' – that is, private discussions where nothing said or conceded can be used later in evidence.

Features of the collaborative process

Some lawyers who practice collaborative law claim that it achieves a win-win outcome and that it allows you to:

▸ maintain control of the process, as well as preserving privacy and dignity

▸ participate in a structured and interest-based negotiation, and

▸ have an open and transparent exchange of all information.

If you are thinking of using this process, consider how realistic these claims are and whether these benefits are likely to occur, or whether they are really to be expected of any lawyer committed to acting in your best interests, regardless of the process followed.

Questions at your first meeting with a lawyer

When you first meet a lawyer, ask as many questions as necessary to assess whether that person is likely to be the right one for you. After all, the relationship might last for many months, sometimes years. You need to have confidence in the lawyer's abilities and competence, and be comfortable about working with him or her for the long haul.

Think about what you want from your lawyer before you meet them. What things are important to you? Are you looking for a lawyer who is likely to:

▸ conduct matters in a constructive and non-confrontational way?

- retain professional objectivity?

- consider the long-term consequences of actions and communications?

- encourage clients to put the best interests of the children first?

- stress the importance of being open and honest?

- encourage all parties to behave in a civilised way?

- keep financial issues separate to children's matters?

- be up front on costs issues – how much you are expected to pay, when and how?

- balance the benefits of any steps against the likely costs – financial and emotional – and maintain a sense of proportionality about your costs?

- inform you of all your options – counselling, family therapy, round-table negotiations, mediation and court proceedings?

- work pro-actively on your matter and focus on results, not the time they spend?

- keep you informed about progress in your matter and relevant dates?

When you meet a family lawyer, ask about these matters and how they approach family law. Try, also, to get a sense of the lawyer's knowledge and skills. You should ask:

- How much will it cost?

- How long will it take?

- What is the lawyer's experience in family law?

- What are your options?

- What is the best plan for your matter?

Work out some realistic and achievable objectives. There is no point starting off with totally unachievable expectations. That's like selecting a real estate agent just because he says he can sell your house for the highest price, regardless of the state of the market.

Assess your lawyer's negotiating skills. Have you found someone who is a listener and prepared to consider all points of view? Or are they dogmatic and opinionated?

If your matter involves complex issues, make sure your lawyer is skilled and experienced in the relevant areas and has dealt before with similar matters.

Always ask the lawyer how they intend to approach your matter – in particular, what's the action plan, how will it be achieved and in approximately what time frame? You want to hire someone who is committed to obtaining achievable and realistic results.

It is pretty meaningless to ask a lawyer about their 'success rates'. Family law is not a win-lose jurisdiction. You would be better off to ask them about their settlement rate – how many of their matters get resolved and within what period of time? Lawyers who talk about family law in win-lose terms might be more inclined to create drawn out confrontations in court, rather than find sensible and reasonable solutions for all parties.

Some lawyers are very busy and may not be able to give your matter the kind of attention it requires. Be wary of those who simply want to pass your matter on to a more junior or less experienced lawyer. It is in your interests to have well-qualified lawyers doing complex legal work, but you may not want to carry the cost of a more accomplished lawyer for the less difficult paperwork involved in a family law matter. There is a balance.

By now, you would have a good impression whether the lawyers you have spoken to have identified the relevant issues in your particular matter and are capable of providing you with sound advice about the issues and your options.

However, at the end of your conversation, you need to assess whether you can relate to that person and whether they relate to you. You're not looking for a new best friend, but you are looking for someone to discuss your family law issues with, honestly and openly.

What your lawyer will want to know

When you go to your first meeting with a lawyer, it really helps if you are prepared and have all of the relevant information available to you.

First, be as clear as possible about the reasons for consulting a lawyer. This sets the tone for your meeting and will enable your lawyer to put their response in context. Are you, for example, seeking general guidance about family law and how it might apply in your case, or are you responding to proceedings that may have commenced or that you want to start.

Secondly, have all the information available that may assist the lawyer, such as financial documents, bank statements and mortgage balances. The more you have, the easier and quicker it will be for the lawyer. Prepare a schedule of your assets and liabilities (as best known to you). If you do not know what bank and credit card accounts you and your partner have, bring any information that is at hand that may assist in tracing those details, such as the names of banks that have been used or details of your ex-partner's employment.

Thirdly, answer all of the lawyer's questions honestly and fully and do not withhold any information that you think might not help your matter. If your lawyer is not told the full position, it is unlikely that the advice you receive will be of full value and may, indeed, be incorrect.

Lastly, tell the lawyer exactly what you want to achieve. What you want may not be achievable but you should give the lawyer an opportunity to consider the possibilities and not guess what you are seeking. Lawyers are not mind readers. If you are not sure what you want, say so.

Objectivity in family law matters

Beware the lawyer who appears to be more than simply compassionate and understanding – the one who starts to identify with the issues and the individuals, who treats the other side as the 'enemy' and who sees family law as a battleground.

It's always nice to have someone who is sympathetic to your issues and understands how tough it is for you. However, there is a danger that a lawyer who becomes overly involved in your matter – and starts to identify with it – may lose objectivity, to the detriment of your best interests.

There are many stories about how family law clients end up paying large sums just to have a lawyer listen patiently to their every problem. Time is money (your money), so use a lawyer to help with your legal problems, not emotional ones.

Your lawyer's job is:

> ▶ to make an objective assessment and advise you of your legal situation

- ▶ to tell you what your options are, and which might be most appropriate to pursue, and

- ▶ to take your instructions and conduct matters with skill and professionalism.

They are not a shoulder for you to cry on. However, if you are finding the emotional fallout from separation difficult, your lawyer should be able to recommend counselling and support services available to you.

After the first meeting

Following your meeting with a prospective lawyer, you should ask for a written initial advice and a case plan setting out how your matter will be conducted, with time and cost estimates. This does not have to be in great detail but should set out the main points of your matter, the advice you have received, the options and proposals to move on, and the anticipated costs.

From these documents, you should learn what your lawyer proposes to do in order to deal with your issues, including:

- ▶ the lawyer's understanding of the relevant information that he or she has received from you

- ▶ the lawyer's legal and strategic advice based on that information

- ▶ the lawyer's understanding of your instructions on how to proceed, and

- ▶ where the matter should progress to from here.

An indication of the lawyer's efficiency is how much time passes before you receive this information. If the lawyer tells you that, due to workload, the information cannot be provided in less than a couple of weeks, move on.

Remember that the lawyer you select will work with you on matters that are probably going to have an impact on you and your family for the rest of your life. So, it is vital that you make a really informed decision to maximise your chances of making the right decision.

When you have decided which lawyer is the one for you, you will be asked to execute a Fee Agreement (covered later in this chapter under 'Lawyers fees' on page 174) and then you are off and running.

Working with your lawyer

Your relationship with your lawyer is governed by professional ethical standards set out by the relevant state regulatory organisation and by the Fee Agreement (or payment contract) you both sign.

However, never forget that you are in charge. You are paying the bills and you are the one who gives the final instructions. Your lawyer can advise and push you in whatever direction they might think is appropriate, but you always call the shots. For example, if you want to settle and your lawyer wants to fight, simply give the order: "Settle" and the lawyer must do all in his or her power to get the matter resolved.

Having said that, there are certain ground rules that apply to your relationship with your lawyer.

Your responsibilities

The Fee Agreement

Read the Fee Agreement carefully to ensure that you know what your obligations are – financial and otherwise.

Disclosure and honesty

You must be honest and disclose all facts and information that might be relevant to your matter. If you do not, your lawyer cannot be held responsible for any negative consequences that might follow. For example, if you fail to disclose you have a bank account overseas, or a drug problem that might impact your capacity to look after your children, and these facts are brought up later, you are unlikely to be seen positively by the court.

Response to requests

You should respond promptly to all requests from your lawyer for information or documents that might be required in court proceedings. If the lawyer cannot prepare for a court hearing or file documents that are required because you have not cleared them, you may face a costs order for not being ready to proceed. The lawyer cannot be blamed for that.

Pay your bills

You should pay all the bills the lawyer sends you in accordance with your agreement. If you have a query about what you have been charged, raise it straight away. If you have problems paying your bills, tell the lawyer so that alternative arrangements might be made. A lawyer is entitled to stop working on your matter if you do not meet your financial obligations, which could leave you in a difficult situation.

Your lawyer's responsibilities

Professionalism and care

Your lawyer has a duty of care to you. They have an obligation to work diligently and professionally on your matter and you should be advised of anything that affects that responsibility. For example, you must be advised if your lawyer is ill and unable to attend to the requirements of your case. If your lawyer cannot attend court because of prior commitments, you should be told.

Part of your lawyer's duty is to ensure that you are kept informed about relevant dates and deadlines – for example, when you have to attend court, or swear or affirm documents. Your lawyer should always keep ahead of the planning in your case and keep you advised of what is going on.

Obviously your lawyer has a responsibility to advise you accurately about the law and about your rights and responsibilities under that law. This advice should be specific and sufficiently detailed so that you understand which laws apply and what the effect of those laws is on your case. For example:

> ▸ If you have received a significant inheritance immediately prior to your separation, your lawyer should advise how the financial provisions of the *Family Law Act* will affect your entitlement to keep the proceeds of this inheritance.

> ▸ If you intend to take your children to live with you overseas, your lawyer should make you aware of the impact of family law on such a decision.

Copies of correspondence and documents

Your lawyer should keep you advised of all relevant communications, such as letters to and from the other party, copies of court documents and orders of the court. These should be sent to you very soon after they have been sent or received – not months later.

Confirm instructions

Your lawyer should always seek or confirm your instructions about running your matter. They must ask for your instructions about offers to settle, or possible court orders that might be made by consent. Don't forget that you are in charge and your lawyer must get your instructions on the major decisions.

Lawyer's fees

Fee Agreements

If you engage a lawyer, you will almost certainly be asked to enter into an agreement with the legal firm about your costs. The agreement may be called a Retainer Agreement, a Legal Costs Agreement, a Fee Agreement, or something along those lines. Such an agreement is compulsory if your lawyer proposes to charge you fees other than those set by 'the scale' (see also the box 'Fee scales' that follows on page 175), which will be in a significant majority of situations. Without your signature on the agreement, the lawyer's costs will be assessed by reference to the rate set out in the scale.

The law accepts that lawyers are entitled to charge at rates higher than the scale, and in accordance with the complexity of the work they undertake, their experience and qualifications (including accredited specialisation), and other commercial considerations. However, it is always wise to carefully check the rates proposed by the lawyer in the Fee Agreement. In all cases, the legal fees must be fair and reasonable and the work done must be appropriate to what is required.

This agreement is a legal document once it has been signed by the lawyer and the client. You have liabilities under it. So, if you have any doubts or concerns, get further legal advice from an independent lawyer about what you are agreeing to do. Make sure you know your financial liabilities and how you are expected to pay the fees – monthly, or as particular events occur, or when the whole matter has finished.

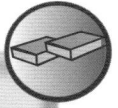

FEE SCALES

Each of the courts where family law is conducted has its own 'scale' for legal fees. These scales set out the basic fees for each item lawyers charge for, including the hourly rates – if that is how work on your matter is being costed. You may check each scale at the relevant court website:

Family Court
www.austlii.edu.au/au/legis/cth/consol_reg/flr2004163/sch3.html

Federal Magistrates Court
www.fmc.gov.au/pubs/html/costs_fl.html

Family Court of Western Australia
As with the Family Court (see above).

Recovering costs

If you can obtain an order that the other party has to pay some or all of your costs, the amount that you can receive is usually determined by the scale rates. Therefore, only very rarely will you get back the same amount that you paid to your lawyer – even when the court has awarded costs.

For example, if the court awards you the costs of a one-hour hearing that your lawyer has charged you $400 per hour for, you will normally only be able to recover the scale fee of, say, $250 per hour. In other words, you will still be out of pocket by $150, even though you were successful.

Over an 18-24 month period it might take for a matter to get right through the litigation process, this difference could be very significant – that is, if you manage to get costs orders along the way.

Paying the other party's costs

If you do not conduct your case in a reasonable manner, you may be ordered to pay some or all of the legal costs of the other party.

For example, if you fail to attend court hearings and the matter is delayed as a result, the court may make an order that you pay the other person's legal costs for that hearing. Or, if the court finds that your claims are totally unrealistic, a costs order against you is possible. This might also happen if you waste the court's time by filing documents that are inaccurate, argumentative or irrelevant.

These are other reasons why having a lawyer to represent you might be worthwhile. A lawyer will at least guide you through the procedural requirements; ensure that your claims are appropriate and that your documents are acceptable. This does not guarantee success, but it might assist you to avoid the expensive consequences of misconceived claims and poor documentation.

Your lawyer's responsibilities in relation to costs

Your lawyer has a legal obligation to keep you informed about your legal costs.

When you are asked to enter into a Fee Agreement, your lawyer must give you an estimate of your costs for the work they will undertake for you. Take this opportunity to ask questions about the costs. For example, when a lawyer gives you an estimate such as "between $5,000 and $50,000", you are entitled to ask why the range is so large. You should probably assume the worst – work out whether you really can afford the upper limit and whether it is justified in your cost-benefit analysis. There may be good reasons why the range is very wide but it does not hurt to ask and understand where the lawyer is coming from.

Whenever an offer to settle is made, your lawyer must also advise you how much you have incurred in legal fees up to that time and how much more might be required to complete the matter.

Your lawyer is also required to give you an update on your costs position whenever a significant court event takes place, such as a conciliation conference or the start of your trial.

Cost updates must also be provided by your lawyer if they become aware of any significant event that could impact on the estimates or quote you have already been given.

These requirements are in place to protect clients who might not know what costs they are liable to pay in the Family Court process. You should insist on your right to be fully informed.

Not happy with your lawyer?

You may have legitimate cause for complaint about your lawyer. Your complaints might be about over charging and legal costs, your lawyer's level of competence, their failure to keep you properly informed, unprofessional conduct, such as not telling you the correct information about your case, a general lack of organisation and inability to manage your case, or a refusal to communicate properly (for example, persistently failing to return your calls and correspondence). A common complaint is that lawyers do not communicate promptly,

If so, you can move on

Firstly, lay your cards on the table and speak to your lawyer. There is no point in just grumbling about the situation or feeling that you are not getting value for the fees you are paying. If your lawyer does not provide satisfactory answers to your concerns, you can always change lawyers. You can ask to be transferred to another lawyer within the same firm, or ask for a final account, pay it and take your files to someone else. However, consider carefully before taking this action – your new lawyer will have to learn everything about your file in order to represent you properly and there may be a significant cost in the process.

Always check how much your new lawyer intends to charge you for this refresher, as it may be quite costly if the matter has been going for a while. These costs may be justified where your current lawyer is not achieving timely results or shows incompetence in handling your matter. Sometimes a new lawyer will agree to take on the matter without charging a refresher fee. If this is the case, make sure the agreement is documented.

Complaints about costs

Sometimes the bills you receive can give rise to a complaint.

This can be a difficult area, as payment on the basis of hourly rates can be pretty open ended. For example, who is to say a particular document should have only taken two hours to draft instead of the five hours that you were charged? Hourly rates are often criticised because they tend to reward the slower and less competent lawyers. Just because one lawyer's hourly rate is lower than the next does not guarantee that your total fees will be less. In fact, they may be a whole lot more.

Challenging an account means that your lawyer should have to provide evidence of the time spent on your matter. However, the outcome is often unpredictable, as the test is whether the work undertaken was both necessary and the time taken was reasonable.

If you do not get reasonable satisfaction from your lawyer about a costs complaint, you can take the matter further and make a formal complaint to the relevant state costs body to have the costs independently assessed.

COMPLAINTS ABOUT COSTS

Information about cost complaints are covered in the following websites

South Australia
www.legalcomplaints.com.au/responding-to-a-complaint/complaints-about-costs

Western Australia
www.legalcosts.wa.gov.au/

New South Wales
www.lawsociety.com.au/idc/groups/public/documents internetcostguidebook/008748.pdf

Victoria
www.liv.asn.au/Getting-Legal-Advice/Choosing-a-Lawyer/Legal-Practitioner-s-Costs

Tasmania
taslawsociety.asn.au/web/en/lawsociety/about/Legal-Profession-Act-2007/ mainColumnParagraphs/01/document/Yourrighttochallengelegalcosts.pdf

Queensland
www.lsc.qld.gov.au/29.htm

Complaints about your lawyer

If your concerns about your lawyer are not cost related, and are not dealt with to your satisfaction by your lawyer, you have three choices:

▶ Forget it and move on.

▶ Report the matter to the responsible authority that regulates lawyers (see the box 'Complaints about lawyers' below).

▶ Seek legal advice about whether you have a cause of action in the courts against your lawyer.

COMPLAINTS ABOUT LAWYERS

New South Wales
www.lawsociety.com.au/community/makingacomplaint/index.htm

Victoria
www.legalaid.vic.gov.au/689.htm

Western Australia
www.legalaid.wa.gov.au/InformationAboutTheLaw/legalproblem/lawyers/Pages/Complaintsaboutlawyers.aspx

Northern Territory
lawsocietynt.asn.au/legal-profession-regulation/complaints-against-lawyers

Queensland
www.lsc.qld.gov.au/171.htm

Western Australia
www.legalcomplaints.com.au/

Tasmania
www.lpbt.com.au/making-a-complaint/

Doing it yourself

No family lawyer can **guarantee** the result that you want. No lawyer can promise that the matter will not go to court. However, if having a lawyer saves you time, gets your issues resolved legally and comes at a reasonable cost, you may decide that this advice and representation really is worthwhile. If not, you should do it yourself.

If you do your own case, you will have to do all the work, from beginning to end, that would normally be done by a lawyer. This includes preparing documents, filing them in court, communications with the other party and generally keeping the case moving.

You will also have to be your own barrister and appear for yourself in preliminary negotiations, hearings in court and in conferences and meetings to discuss the matter.

Can you do it yourself?

Yes! Of course you can. It won't cost anything, as you don't charge yourself legal fees.

Nothing prevents anyone from being their own lawyer, drafting up their own documents, complying with the court's requirements and representing themselves in court.

However, it is a very time-consuming process and there are pitfalls. For a start, you may be too close to the issues and this may affect your objectivity. It is very difficult to disassociate yourself from the rights and wrongs, especially if you are one of the involved parties.

The processes involved in 'running' a children's or property case are well known to a family lawyer. This does not mean that you cannot learn them, but it will take time and you can make many mistakes.

You will have to do all your own preparation and documentation, you may have to interview witnesses and prepare court documents for your witnesses and you will certainly have to gather all of the evidence that may be relevant to your matter and present it in the best possible light.

At trial, you will also have to deal with the evidence of the other side in accordance with family law rules and the applicable rules of evidence. For example, you will have to have an understanding of the rules relating to cross examination, admissible evidence, relevance and other legal and technical issues.

The steps you will have to undertake

Negotiation and pre-litigation processes

You can do your own negotiating and you can come to an agreement that you may then wish to put into a legally binding document that is filed in the courts.

The court websites will help you with these processes and with the documents that are required. However, if you do them yourself, you 'alone' are responsible for the results and, if you haven't covered everything you should have, you may find yourself back in court, anyway, with an argument about whether the document is binding or not.

COURT WEBSITES FOR SETTLEMENT

Family Court of Australia
www.familylawcourts.gov.au/wps/wcm/connect/FLC/Home/Forms/Do-it-yourself+kits/FCOA_form_diy_App_Consent_Orders

Federal Magistrates Court
www.familylawcourts.gov.au/wps/wcm/connect/FLC/Home/Forms/Do-it-yourself+kits/

Family Court of Western Australia
www.familycourt.wa.gov.au/K/kits.aspx

Litigation processes

The litigation process is covered in detail in chapter 8 'If it positively, definitely has to go to court', including lots of handy hints about what is required to work through the court process.

Trial

If your matter goes all the way to a trial (and, remember, only about 10 per cent of all cases get that far), it will demand a lot of preparation and a thorough understanding of what evidence might be required to establish the case you are presenting.

At this stage, you are not only your own lawyer but you have to be a barrister as well.

BARRISTERS – WHO THEY ARE AND WHAT THEY DO

When someone with a law degree finishes law school, they are not automatically a qualified lawyer. In order to become a lawyer, they need to pass additional exams and spend supervised time in a legal workplace. A lawyer may then choose to specialise and become a 'barrister'.

Barristers are lawyers who have decided to focus on the specific legal task of representing clients in court proceedings and advise on complex legal issues. They may also run mediations and do other tasks. However, their main focus is turning up in court to argue cases.

Your lawyer may represent you at interim hearings in court, where the issues are short and often procedural but, when you get to the trial stage, your lawyer is likely to suggest taking on a barrister to represent you.

Why hire a barrister? Why not have your lawyer stand up and speak for you throughout the trial? After all, they've gotten you this far.

Hiring a barrister is usually a good idea for trial and for more complex hearings. This is because a good barrister:

> ▸ *will be an excellent public speaker, trained to be convincing, clear and argue well*
> ▸ *will have an excellent working knowledge of the law, particluarly the laws relating to evidence – what may, and may not, be said in court*
> ▸ *will be trained to examine and cross examine witnesses and have considerable experience in this art (it's harder than it looks on TV!)*
> ▸ *will be aware of the workings of the rules of the court – and will know when to object if the other side is doing something inappropriate, and*
> ▸ *will be adept at the art of directing the discussion. They will encourage everyone in the court room to focus on things that are good for your case, while brushing over the things that perhaps do not make you look so good.*

Of course, not all barristers have all of these skills to the same high level, but a good barrister will be able to do all of these things.

Presenting your case at trial is not what you see on *LA Law* or *Judge Judy*. If you don't have at least a basic understanding of the rules of evidence and court procedures, you may find yourself at a significant disadvantage – especially if the other party has legal representation. Good barristers are not only clever with words and quick on their feet, they are usually very knowledgeable about the rules and know what can and can't be put to the court.

They are also aware of the nuances of the case as it progresses. They know when to shift their position to counter the other party's arguments as they emerge. They also have the ability to exploit weaknesses through cross examination.

If you are going to represent yourself, we suggest you do three things:

> ▸ read all of the rules of court very carefully
>
> ▸ research the rules of evidence that apply in the court where you are going to appear – different rules of evidence apply in different courts, and

> ▸ visit the court before your case and watch other trials and proceedings being conducted to get a feel for how matters progress.

Judges – especially in the Family Courts – are tolerant of some mistakes, but not where they repeatedly tie up the court process and waste court time.

DO-IT-YOURSELF TIPS

There are guidelines for representing yourself in the Family Court, which you must read if you do not intend to use a lawyer:

**www.familylawcourts.gov.au/wps/wcm/connect/FLC/Home/
About+Going+to+Court/Applying+to+the+courts/**

You should also consider the following:

▶   *Even if you don't turn up to court, this doesn't prevent the judge from making orders against you.*

▶   *Filing lots of documents in court will not necessarily cover all the bases and make you look good, even if you think it will. You should only file relevant documents. Cross examining your ex will not be like when you used to argue with them at home. Regardless of what points you may think you have scored, the judge is only going to take into account facts that are relevant in deciding your case.*

▶   *The judge will not give you any legal advice. The lawyer from the other side won't give you any legal advice. This may seem obvious but, when you are in court and trying to conduct your case, you may find you are confused by what is going on. The people around you are not permitted to give you advice on how to proceed. If you find yourself in this position, you should consider talking to a duty lawyer (for free), if there is one available at the court you are in.*

▶   *Just because you refuse to sign a document, it doesn't mean that matters cannot proceed. In some circumstances, judges have the power to sign documents on your behalf. For example, if you refuse to sign a child's passport documents, the court may do it for you; this might also happen if you refuse to sign property transfer papers that have been ordered by the court.*

THE ELEPHANT IN THE ROOM
– LEGAL COSTS IN FAMILY LAW MATTERS

SUMMARY

▸ Legal fees in family law matters can be expensive.

▸ Lawyers are engaged in over 80 per cent of Family Court matters.

▸ You don't only have to pay for your lawyer's time – you will also have to pay for the expenses that your lawyer makes on your behalf (photocopying charges, hiring experts to value your house, engaging a barrister) and court fees and charges.

▸ Family law is not the kind of law where the loser pays. Instead, unless there are unusual circumstances, each person pays their own costs. Even if you get what you want in the end, you will still have to pay your lawyer.

▸ The legal fees you pay may end up being more expensive than the dollar difference you are arguing over. It may come down to a question of whether you would rather give the money to a lawyer or share it with your ex.

▸ It is very difficult to get free legal advice or support. Legal Aid is only available in limited circumstances for children's matters, not financial cases, and community legal services are always stretched for resources.

▸ Most family lawyers charge by the hour. Some firms may offer fixed fee plans for your family law matter.

The high cost of family law matters

It will come as no surprise to hear that legal costs in the Family Courts can be very high.

Reports of family law cases where the legal fees cost each party hundreds of thousands of dollars are not uncommon. On the other hand, many matters also resolve quickly and without great expense.

Apart from the media, no one seems to like talking about legal costs. Lawyers can be unhelpful about likely future fees and clients often don't want to hear about them anyway. Legal costs are 'the elephant in the room', the subject that everyone pretends is not there in the vain hope that the problem will go away. Regrettably, the issue does not go away, so it may as well be addressed fully at the first opportunity.

Different fee arrangements

There are three common arrangements to pay legal fees in family law:

▸ you pay according to the costs scale, a scale of fees set by each court

▸ you pay according to an hourly rate, set by your lawyer, or

▸ you pay according to a fixed-fee agreement with your lawyer.

Scale fees

Scale fees are the rates set out in a fixed schedule of costs regulated by the relevant court (explained in the box 'fee scales' on page 175).

Not many lawyers will charge according to the scale rates, but some do and these charges are usually much less than other fee arrangements.

Time-based fees

Time-based fees are when you are charged on the basis of the time spent by your lawyer. Your lawyer's 'hourly rate' (how much they charge for each hour of work they perform) is multiplied by the amount of time they spend on your matter to arrive at the amount you have to pay.

Fixed fees

Fixed fees are arrangements you have with your lawyer before any work begins, about what will be charged for undertaking the agreed work.

Which fee method to choose

There may be advantages and disadvantages in each of the fee arrangements.

Hopefully, the difficulties of comparing the different arrangements – a bit like trying to compare apples with oranges – may become clearer as you read the rest of this chapter.

Questions to ask about legal costs in family law

Apart from the question about which fee arrangement might apply to your case, there are several vital issues you should understand about legal costs in family law:

- ▶ What are you paying for?
- ▶ How much will it cost you?
- ▶ Who pays the costs?
- • When are they paid?
- • How are they paid?

What are you paying for?

Depending on which fee arrangement applies in your case, you will normally have to pay for:

- ▶ your lawyer's time
- ▶ your lawyer's disbursements (expenses and payments made on your behalf), and
- ▶ court fees and charges.

Your lawyer's time

It is really important for anyone who proposes to use a lawyer to know how a lawyer charges fees and how they calculate their bills. After all, you are the one who has to pay them.

Most lawyers who work in family law will charge you according to the amount of time they spend on your matter, which is often called 'time billing' or 'time-based fees'. If a lawyer proposes to charge you more than the scale fee (and most do), the lawyer should have an agreement with you setting out what the rates are.

With time billing, the actual fee charged is calculated by multiplying the lawyer's hourly rate by the amount of time spent working on your matter. If a lawyer has a hourly rate of $350 and spends 10 hours working on your matter, you will be charged $3,500. If you had a lawyer with an hourly rate of $400, your bill for the same hours of work would be $4,000. The bills are simply a measure of the amount of time your lawyer has spent working on your case – regardless of the result.

So, when you go to see a lawyer who tells you that their hourly rate is $X, they are not telling you how much the matter will cost, they are just telling you what you have to pay for every hour of their time.

Many lawyers will give you estimates (and family lawyers are required to do so when a matter goes to court), but an estimate is exactly that. Most of these estimates will have a large range between the upper and lower figures as it can be difficult to estimate what a matter will cost over the whole journey.

Different hourly rates do not necessarily assist in working out how big or small your bill will be. A lawyer charging $500 an hour might be an absolute gun and do a particular job in much less time than a less experienced (but still competent) lawyer who charges, say, $300 an hour. Different hourly rates may help you to assess a lawyer's relative experience (and expense), but this knowledge does not enable you to calculate what your legal costs will be at the end of the day. You might actually spend a lot less with a lawyer who has a higher hourly billing rate.

What is included in time?

Although most lawyers charge by the time they spend on your matter, it is important to know what is included in 'chargeable time' and what is not. As a rule, they charge for work that is 'necessary' and 'reasonable'. This could include:

▸ attending meetings and conferences

▸ taking instructions from you

▸ taking evidence from people involved in your case

- ▶ preparing before meetings, or preparing notes afterwards

- ▶ considering (thinking about) and researching issues to do with your matter

- ▶ discussing your matter on the telephone (with you or anyone else)

- ▶ preparing and sending letters, faxes and/or emails (to you or anyone else)

- ▶ reading and considering letters, faxes and/or emails (from you or anyone else)

- ▶ copying letters, faxes and/or emails to you or others who might be involved in your case

- ▶ looking at documents provided by you or by others and taking copies or making notes about those documents

- ▶ preparing documents for court or for hearings

- ▶ attending hearings in court or mediations

- ▶ meeting with a barrister to discuss your matter or preparing documents for the barrister

- ▶ waiting for a hearing to start in court, or for a mediation or a conference

- ▶ travelling to and from the court for meetings or conferences, and

- ▶ discussing your matter with someone else (personally, or on the telephone)

Whatever time the lawyer spends on these activities (or is spent by other people engaged by the lawyer) will be charged to you.

Fixed fees in family law

Fixed fees are pretty simple. You and your lawyer discuss a plan for your matter, the work required to execute that plan and the amount to be paid for that work. You then discuss how you will pay for the agreed costs. If you reach agreement, you sign a contract and the lawyer gets working.

Fixed fees may not be everyone's cup of tea. For example, if you have a case with complicated ownership issues in companies and trusts all over the place, or where complex and uncertain legal issues need to be resolved, a fixed fee may not be offered to you.

Advantages of fixed fees

The advantages of a fixed fee arrangement in your family law matter are pretty straight forward:

▶ you know up front exactly what your costs will be

▶ you can make realistic arrangements about how and when to pay your legal bills, and

▶ you will pay a fee that equals the value you and your lawyer place on the work to be done, not the time it may take.

Comparing fixed fees with hourly rates – apples and oranges

Can you compare a fixed fee arrangement with the initial estimates that are given where an hourly rate is being used? Unfortunately not. They are totally different practices and are based on entirely different principles.

With fixed fees: you know what you are getting yourself into **before** you start the engagement and, therefore, you have certainty about the price you will pay.

With hourly rates: you can only know **after** the engagement what you have to pay. You get an estimate (which may or may not turn out to be accurate). The cost will be determined by the amount of time your lawyer takes to complete your matter.

Disbursements

You are also required to pay 'disbursements'. These are expenses incurred on your behalf, other than the fees you pay for lawyers' time. These costs are payable by you if you are being charged on a time billing arrangement and may or may not be included in a fixed fee agreement.

Typically, these costs include:

▶ fees charged for work done by other professionals (for example, barristers, experts, valuers, psychologists)

▶ costs incurred while managing a matter, such as courier fees, and

▶ 'soft' disbursements, such as photocopying, telephone charges, faxes and emails.

If a lawyer proposes to engage an accounting expert on your behalf, make sure you have a pretty good idea of their likely fees before you agree. Expert accountants often charge fees in the tens of thousands. Like lawyers, they normally charge for their time on an hourly basis, rather than having fixed and pre-agreed fees.

The cost of barristers

If your lawyer wishes to engage a barrister to represent you in court, or to obtain an opinion about your matter, you should ask why this is necessary and what the likely costs will be. Barristers can provide great opinions – which help you to understand how your matter is likely to pan out – but be aware that barristers may also charge at an hourly rate. You will be asked to pay whatever the barrister charges.

Court fees and charges

Court fees are usually also described as a disbursement – a cost you will have to pay. The fees for filing documents in court and for hearings are all set out on the relevant court websites. These are almost always paid before the event or when filing documents.

You may qualify for a reduction in fees in some instances, so it is worth checking whether or not this is the case with the courts.

FEES IN THE COURTS

Federal Magistrates Court
www.fmc.gov.au/html/fees_family.html

Family Court
www.familylawcourts.gov.au/wps/wcm/connect/FLC/Home/Fees/Court+fees/

Family Court of Western Australia
www.familycourt.wa.gov.au/F/fees_and_forms.aspx?uid=9339-7089-1873-0177

So, how much will my matter cost?

The actual cost of each matter will depend upon a range of factors including:

▶ the fee arrangement you choose

▶ the complexity of your matter

▶ the efficiency and effectiveness of your legal representation, and

▶ how quickly you can get the matter resolved.

Where any of these factors is unknown, it is difficult to work out precisely what your fees will be. That is why lower and upper ranges may vary widely.

Ranges of fees

In family law matters where you are being charged according to the time spent on your case, your lawyer should give you an estimate of how much it will cost to do the work you require. However, these estimates are not the final word and your bill may exceed the original estimate by a significant amount. That is not necessarily the lawyer's fault as matters can blow out in unexpected ways. However, the bigger the estimated range, the more careful you should be. Ask the lawyer to step you through the estimate and explain the ranges quoted.

The extent of the range may reflect the fact that there are significant unknowns in your case.

A lawyer is required to update you with details about your fees on a regular basis and you are always entitled to ask for their estimates of future costs and likely disbursements.

With fixed fees, you will know how much you have to pay at each stage of the work that is required and estimates are likely to be given only for work in the future that may or may not be required.

Your best chance of minimising the overall costs (and keeping them at the lower end of the estimated range), is to get the matter settled as early as possible. This is because with time billing, the longer it goes on, the more hours that the lawyer puts in, meaning that it is more likely the upper limits of the estimated range will be tested.

Who pays the costs in family law matters?

Family law is not a 'loser pays' jurisdiction, unlike most other civil jurisdictions. In the Family Courts, each party pays their own costs.

Again – although this is not an absolute rule – it is safe to assume you will have to pay your own legal costs in the vast majority of cases. Therefore, you must carefully consider the costs you will incur and the financial impact of running a legal case.

Costs orders

A costs order is where one party has to pay some (and in some circumstances, all) of the other person's legal costs. Costs orders may be made against the other party in situations such as:

▸ you being wholly successful in the proceedings (in other words, you got what you asked for and the other party did not)

▸ you made an offer to settle that was very reasonable and that offer was rejected by the other side. or

▸ the other party's conduct of the case left a lot to be desired.

When a costs order is made, the party who has to pay generally pays the scale costs – that is, the rate set out in a fixed schedule of costs regulated by each court (explained in the box 'Fee scales' on page 175). Generally, if you are being paid costs by the other party, you will not get back everything you have paid your lawyer – and perhaps only 50-60 per cent of what you have paid.

Very infrequently, the court will make an order for what is known as 'indemnity costs', where one party is ordered to pay the actual costs that the other paid to their lawyer.

It is not common to get a costs order, especially an indemnity costs order, against the other party in the family law system.

Don't bank on getting a costs order in your favour at the end of your matter. If you do, it is more than likely you will be disappointed.

Proportionality

Try to keep a sense of proportion between the likely cost of family law matters and the potential outcome of taking a matter to the Family Court. In other words, weigh up what you are arguing about against the likely costs of that argument. This is a less difficult task where the argument is about property.

Take a simple example:

> ▸ you have total property worth $250,000 (after deducting all your debts)

> ▸ you want a 60:40 split in your favour ($150,000 for you)

> ▸ your ex-partner wants a 50:50 split ($125,000 for you), and

> ▸ you are 10 per cent apart ($25,000).

Each party's lawyer estimates that taking it to court will cost $30,000. Together, you are spending $60,000 to have an argument over $25,000.

> ▸ If you win, you end up with $120,000 ($150,000, less $30,000 costs).

> ▸ If you lose, you end up with $95,000 ($125,000, less $30,000 costs).

You could have compromised at the start for the amount that the other person was offering and been better off. Now, that is a true lose-lose outcome.

Therefore, it often makes sense to look for a compromise solution that does not expose everyone to potentially crippling legal costs.

It is impossible to put a value on the effective resolution of children's matters, but one financial aspect of the outcome is predictable – everyone loses.

No tax deductions for legal fees

Legal fees in family law matters are not tax deductible. Family law legal fees are paid from 'after tax' money earned from your jobs or investments. Think of this when you consider the commitment to commence proceedings in the Family Courts.

So, negotiate, mediate and arbitrate. Do whatever it takes to come to reasonable agreements, and hold onto your hard-earned money.

When must fees be paid?

Like everyone in business, your lawyer must be paid. How and when you must make the payments is a vital discussion that you must have with your lawyer at the earliest possible moment.

With time billing, you usually receive a bill from your lawyer at the end of each month. It will set out what work has been done and how much you have to pay.

With fixed fees, you would normally receive your bill after each quoted stage of the work has been completed.

The payment options will depend entirely on the agreement you reach with your lawyer.

Monthly fees

In most circumstances, your lawyer will expect you to pay your account in full each month – from whatever sources might be available to you. Most lawyers expect payment within 30 days and may stop working on your matter if the money does not arrive by then.

Up-front fees

Some lawyers will want you to pay into their Trust Account a fixed sum of money or an amount equal to their estimate for the total amount of work, before they even start work.

THE TRUST ACCOUNT

Money on trust

This is payment 'on trust' into a lawyer's Trust Account before starting work on your matter is not unusual.

You are providing the lawyer with the best kind of security that they will be paid after their services have been delivered – particularly where you are paying an open-ended hourly rate. When you put your money into the lawyer's Trust Account, it remains there until drawn out to pay their fees and costs as they are billed.

Covering disbursements

Almost all lawyers require you to pay some money into their Trust Account to cover them for 'disbursements' they are likely to incur. For example, if a court hearing is coming up and a barrister has been briefed, the lawyer may ask you for the full amount of the barrister's estimated costs to be paid into their Trust Account before the barrister starts work. Similarly, if a valuation is required, your lawyer will want the cost of that valuation paid into the Trust Account so they can pay the valuer as soon as the report is provided.

Pay-at-the-end (PATE)

Whether time billing or charging fixed fees, some lawyers will allow you to pay your fees at the end of the matter (and may charge you interest). In these circumstances, the lawyer will want some form of security for the payment, such as a mortgage over real estate or a guarantee from a third party. If the lawyer is 'carrying' you in this way (effectively being a bank by lending you the money), it is not unreasonable that they should want these securities or that they should charge interest.

How are you going to pay your legal costs?

Whether you are paying up front each month or at the end of your matter, it is pointless engaging lawyers if you are unable or unwilling to pay for their services.

Legal fees have to be paid – whether from your wages, a draw-down on investments, sale of a property or a business or shares, from savings or borrowings through a credit card, personal loan, overdraft or money lent to you by a relative or friend.

So, at the time you decide to engage a lawyer, you should discuss exactly how the payment will be made.

Legal Aid and free services

There is very little financial assistance available for a family law case.

You may find local legal services that provide pro-bono (free) assistance – but this is likely to be available only in limited circumstances and if you are in a very difficult financial position. You can also ask a lawyer if they are prepared to take on your case on a pro-bono basis. It is an unlikely outcome, but you may be lucky.

If you cannot afford a lawyer at all but you need legal assistance, you may be eligible for a grant of legal aid (see the box 'Advice about Legal Aid' below). Some will qualify for assistance from the Aboriginal Legal Service.

ADVICE ABOUT LEGAL AID

National Association of Community Legal Centres
www.naclc.org.au

State-based organisations

ACT:	www.legalaidact.org.au
NSW:	www.legalaid.nsw.gov.au/asp/index.asp
NT:	www.ntlac.nt.gov.au/
QLD:	www.legalaid.qld.gov.au/Pages/Home.aspx
SA:	www.lsc.sa.gov.au/
TAS:	www.legalaid.tas.gov.au/
VIC:	www.legalaid.vic.gov.au/
WA:	www.legalaid.wa.gov.au/Pages/Default.aspx

Aboriginal & Torres Strait Islanders Legal Assistance
https://nwjc.org.au/atisla.html

Legal funding loans

Another option is to seek a loan from a third party – generally a litigation funding company that provides you with the funds to meet your legal expenses (and, sometimes, also to help with your living expenses).

This will come at a cost:

> ▸ Fees will be payable to establish the loan and interest will be charged.

> ▸ The lender will require security over a property in which you have an interest (to ensure that there is a source of payment if you cannot repay the loan at the end of the matter).

> ▸ Usually you repay all of the loan plus the fees after all of the proceedings have been finalised.

> ▸ If you do not repay whatever is owing, the security may be sold to pay the loan and the costs of enforcing the loan agreement.

Other credit arrangements for legal fees

Using a credit card, obtaining a guarantee or arranging a loan facility from your bank are also options for the payment of legal fees.

Competitive credit card interest rates can be found and, where you have security in real estate, bank guarantees can be an affordable option. If you are in such a position, ask your bank to give you a price on a guarantee.

If you are unable to negotiate an early settlement, you may have to approach relatives and friends to assist you with payment of your legal fees.

Where you have to borrow money to pay fees, this may be taken into account in the final property distribution. However, it is only a likely scenario where the other party has the means to pay their legal costs and, without the loan, you do not.

MYTHS AND REALITY IN FAMILY LAW

Over time, many myths have grown around family law. We all know someone who has been involved in family disputes and they all have a horror story to tell – many get much better in the telling.

The particular laws that apply in this area are updated and changed quite frequently and this can lead to misunderstandings about what happens when couples separate. Recent changes – particularly around de facto relationships and arrangements for children – have added to these misunderstandings.

Media reports often focus on sensationalist aspects of family law cases ('Mistress claims assets', 'Family Court awards father equal time', 'Mother forced to live in remote town to see children'), which can create even further misconceptions in the public mind.

What follows are some examples of common misunderstandings — and the reality.

Fault at separation

> *If the separation is one person's 'fault' – for example, because they had an affair or abandoned the family – they will be punished and the other person may get more of the property or more time with the children.*

It doesn't work that way, as unfair as it may seem. Family law in Australia looks primarily to the future – what you will need in the future (financially) and what arrangements can be made for your children that are in their best interests. Although you may be hurt by the actions of your ex, there are no legal provisions to 'punish' them by giving you more in the division of money or time with children.

Family law is a 'no fault' jurisdiction and questions of morality do not come into decisions.

Custody of pets

We can get orders in court to both have time (or 'share custody' in the American phrasing) with our dog/cat/goldfish.

'Fluffy' may be part of your family but the law sees pets as property, not as people. After all, Fluffy can't say who she wants to live with!

Property is divided between the two people involved – legally, your pet will belong to one or other of you after separation, and orders will not be made for you to 'share time' with the pet.

Of course, you can come to a non-legal arrangement between yourselves about time sharing with your pet and carry it out yourselves. However, if there is an argument between you about time with the pet, the only way a court can solve it is by allocating the pet to one of you, solely as part of the property division.

Listening to kids

The kids have said they only want to live with me and they don't want to see their Dad/Mum. The court has to listen to them, right?

This depends on the age of your children. If they are not teenagers, other considerations will probably carry more weight. If the children are older and show maturity, the court will give more weight to their opinions. Especially as children reach the age of 15 or 16, it is difficult to force them to spend time with a parent they do not want to spend time with.

The Family Courts are very good at assessing whether an opinion is a child's own opinion or something that their parent has talked them into saying. If you try to influence your children's views and this becomes known, the judge will not think much of your abilities as a parent. If there is any question about what your children really think and why, the court may have a child expert speak to them alone, find out what they think and report back to the court.

It's against Dads

Family law is prejudiced against Dads. Mum will automatically get more time with the children if the case goes to court.

This is not true, however there are reasons why it may seem to be.

Studies have shown that young children (under the age of five or six) need the stability of living consistently with one parent – sharing that involves different evenings in different places is not necessarily in their best interests. However, it is good for children to have frequent time during the day with the other parent to maintain their relationship.

Because of the physical bond a mother has with a child after birth, she will usually be the parent that a very young child stays with.

When they are at school age, children cope much better with time sharing between parents and more equal time-sharing arrangements might be appropriate.

It may seem unfair that one parent gets more time with younger children than the other, but don't forget – the law prioritises children's best interests over parents' best interests.

The best position on separation

Now that we're separated, my ex will be able to take all my money because the kids mostly live with her.

OR

Now that we're separated, my ex will get to keep all the money because he's the breadwinner and I won't be able to support the kids.

Neither of these is true.

Nobody will get to keep "all the money" – not you and not your ex either. Instead, the law tries to ensure that both are financially supported, with the amount and method of support depending on the circumstances in each case.

Provision for the kids through child support can be sorted out in a number of ways. If you are worried that your partner used to support you financially and now you don't have any source of income, you may want to investigate applying for spousal maintenance (even if you were not married).

Allegations of abuse

If a mother makes allegations of abuse against a father, she will be believed and he will be punished by not being allowed to see his children.

The Family Courts are very good at assessing the difference between real and false allegations of abuse.

The court will look at what is said by witnesses in court, as well as evidence such as police records, doctors' and hospital records, reports from schools and from the State Government department in charge of health and welfare.

People who make up allegations of abuse are looked on very critically by the court. It may even order you to pay some or all of the costs of the other person.

Even if allegations of abuse are found to be true, they don't necessarily mean that the abusive parent will be prevented from seeing their children, although visits may be supervised by an independent person to make sure nothing goes wrong.

Equal time for fathers

The law was changed in 2006 to give fathers the right to have equal time with their children.

The *Family Law Act* presumes that parents should have "equal shared parental responsibility" for their children but this does not mean that they should also have the right to enjoy **equal time** with their children.

The court is now required to consider whether "substantial and significant care" by a parent is appropriate, but decisions will always be based on what is considered in the best interests of the children.

What are assets?

Compensation payments, inheritances and gifts are never included as assets to be distributed if you separate.

Compensation, damages awards and inheritances will normally be included in an asset pool, if they are in existence at the date of reckoning. But inclusion in the pool does not automatically mean the other party is entitled to share in the value of these 'assets'.

The factors taken into account to determine the contribution made by the party who received the compensation, damages or inheritance will vary depending on the circumstances of each case. There may also be an adjustment on account of one or more of the Section 75(2) factors (see under 'The three steps of property distribution' on page 57).

Kids mean more assets

Whoever gets the kids after separation gets at least 60 per cent of the assets.

Family law is a discretionary jurisdiction – meaning that the courts have wide powers to make orders. Many facts are taken into account to determine how assets will be distributed. Parties' contributions and their perceived needs will be assessed. Care arrangements for the children is just one of many matters that will be considered. There are no requirements in family law for fixed percentage distributions in any circumstances.

Natural parents have exclusive rights

Only the natural parents of a child may participate in that child's care and development.

Family law does not prevent people other than natural birth parents from seeking court orders that would enable them to care for a child.

Grandparents regularly make such claims and are, in many cases, successful in having their grandchildren placed in their care by the Family Court.

Rather than rely on popular but wildly inaccurate myths, you should seek legal advice about your rights and responsibilities, your entitlements and your obligations at family law. This is the case whether you are separated after a marriage or your de facto relationship has broken down, whether you are a parent, a grandparent or, simply, a person interested in a child's welfare and development.

RESOURCES

For further information please visit:

www.slatergordon.com.au/flresources

This website provides a detailed and wide range of references and resources under the following headings:

- ▶ Government
- ▶ The courts
- ▶ Mediation
- ▶ Legal help
- ▶ Counselling and support
- ▶ Resources for parents
- ▶ Family violence support
- ▶ Mental health and support services
- ▶ Family law information
- ▶ Adoption
- ▶ Costs
- ▶ The law
- ▶ Child support

GLOSSARY OF TERMS USED IN THIS BOOK

Affidavit

A written statement of fact that its author swears to be true. This document is the equivalent of evidence given verbally in court: it has to be the truth, the whole truth, and nothing but the truth.

Appeals

A court hearing (usually in a superior court) held to challenge the outcome of a previous decision.

Applicant

The person who files the first documents with the court seeking a specific outcome. Those documents are also given to the other party in the proceedings (the respondent –see glossary listing).

Application for Final Orders

A document filed with the court stating what you want it to decide on a final basis.

Application in a case

A document filed with the court stating what you want it to decide on a temporary basis while the arrangements for a final agreement are still being worked out.

Barrister

A lawyer who specialises in court work and complex matters.

Capital Gains Tax (CGT)

CGT may be payable on the profits made on the sale of assets. It is calculated by subtracting the initial cost (plus allowances for inflation increases) from what you receive when you sell or dispose of it. The family home is usually exempt from CGT but investment properties and many other assets that you have acquired may attract the tax.

Child Support Agency	*The government organisation that is responsible for administering the child support scheme and transferring payments from one parent to another.*
Circuit	*A process where a judge or magistrate visits remote, rural or regional areas to hold court hearings.*
Collaborative law	*A method where lawyers commit to negotiating rather than pursuing litigation in court.*
Conciliation conference	*A compulsory conference that is held before an impartial third party who works for the court. This is held prior to your court hearing in an attempt to reach an agreement between the parties and avoid final litigation.*
Consent orders	*Binding orders made by the court with the agreement of both parties. Usually these will have been worked out by the parties and their lawyers outside the court and then a judge or magistrate will approve them.*
Contravention order	*An order made when a previous court order has been breached to fix the problem and/or to punish the person who has breached the order.*
De facto relationship	*The relationship of a couple who live together without being married. This is a grey area – the question of whether any particular couple are in a de facto relationship is still being defined and clarified by decisions of the Family Court.*
Divorce	*The legal process that dissolves a marriage. This can only occur once a couple have been separated for a year.*
Family Court of Australia	*A court that deals exclusively with more complex family law matters, including those involving large asset pools and difficult children's cases.*

Family Court of Western Australia	*The court that deals with family law matters and cases in Western Australia.*
Family law rules	*The rules of the Family Court of Australia that are set by the judges of that court to regulate the procedures and processes for the conduct of family law matters.*
Federal Magistrates Court	*The court that deals with the majority of family law cases in Australia (except WA). Unless the issues are of significant complexity, a family law case is likely to be heard in this court.*
Federal magistrate	*A person with many years' experience in the law who is appointed by the government to determine cases in the Federal Magistrates Court.*
Filing	*The process of providing a document to the court to be added to the court file. These documents need to be formatted correctly and processed by the court in order for a judge to consider them.*
Final orders	*Orders made by the court on a permanent basis.*
Financial Agreement	*(Also sometimes known as 'pre-nups') An agreement made between married or de facto couples before, during, or after the relationship commences. It takes the power away from the court to divide your property. They allow you to make your own decisions about how your property will be divided.*
Financial resource	*Some financial entitlements are not regarded as property in family law but may be taken into account as a resource, such as potential payments from a family company or a claim to an asset that might arise in the future. These will generally be taken into account at step 3 of the property distribution process as an adjustment to one or other party.*

Financial statement	*A document filed with the court in property matters that states the current position of your finances including any and all assets and debts.*
Flagging order	*An order that freezes the distribution or payment of superannuation. This type of order is made to protect the asset until access is agreed.*
Full Court of the Family Court	*A rotating group of three Family Court of Australia judges that meets to decide appeal cases.*
High Court of Australia	*The highest court in Australia that has the final word on family law cases. It is not common for family law cases to be heard in the High Court.*
Interim order	*An order that is made during the progress of your case, to sort out matters that need to be dealt with before the final trial takes place. An interim order is usually only temporarily in place.*
Judge	*A person with many years' experience in the law who is appointed by the government to determine complex cases in the Family Court.*
Litigation	*The process of going to court. This could be a short process, or a very drawn out one, depending on your case.*
Nullity	*An order of the Family Court of Australia that the marriage in question was not legally valid and, as a result, that the parties were never legally married.*
Order	*An order of the courts is a decision which is binding against all parties – it may be in relation to a financial issue, about arrangements for the children or it may be a direction as to how the proceedings will be conducted. An order may be for a limited time (such as, until another order is made or until the next hearing) or it may be final.*

Parties	The people involved in a dispute in court – usually the couple who are no longer together. Other parties to the case may include those who have a financial interest in your property or those with caring responsibilities for children.
Presiding officer	The judge or federal magistrate who oversees your case from start to finish.
Procedural order	An order made by the court about the way your case will progress. This might be giving a date of a hearing, requiring documents to be filed or providing for other administrative and organisational requirements.
Registrar	An experienced family lawyer who is hired by the government to work for the court. They may hold conferences to try to help couples reach an agreement, and also manage some procedural orders. Registrars can also grant divorces.
Registry	Each individual court is described by its 'registry' which is its geographical location, for example, the Melbourne Registry and the Dandenong Registry. Each court operates its own systems within the rules and regulations of family law.
Respondent	The person who receives the documents filed in court by the applicant. This person then has the opportunity to respond to those documents with their own court documents.
Relocation	Where one parent wants to move a long distance away from the other parent (often interstate or overseas) and take the children with them. A parent should not move in this manner without a court order permitting them to do so.

Rules of evidence	*Rules relating to what evidence (including documentary evidence) may be admitted in the courts and what will not. A well-known rule of evidence relates to the inadmissibility of 'hearsay evidence', ie when someone says that they heard something said.*
Rules (of the court)	*The Family Court of Australia and the Federal Magistrates Court have their own rules governing processes and procedures.*
Scale (of costs)	*The scale is the fee, set by regulation, that lawyers may charge for their work. The reasonableness of the legal fees you are to be charged will be referenced to the scale that applies in your court.*
Separation	*The point at which a relationship between two people has irretrievably broken down.*
Splitting order	*An order to divide one person's superannuation between two parties. The superannuation remains inaccessible until you are old enough to receive it.*